This book is from
the kitchen libary of

PETER BRUNS

ALSO BY ART GINSBURG, MR. FOOD®

The Mr. Food® Cookbook, OOH it's so GOOD!!™ (1990)

Mr. Food® Cooks Like Mama (1992)

Mr. Food® Cooks Chicken (1993)

Mr. Food® Cooks Pasta (1993)

Mr. Food® Makes Dessert (1993)

Mr. Food® Cooks Real American (1994)

Mr. Food®'s Favorite Cookies (1994)

Mr. Food®'s Quick and Easy Side Dishes (1995)

Mr. Food® Grills It All in a Snap (1995)

MR. FOOD®'s
Fun Kitchen Tips and Shortcuts
(and Recipes, Too!)

Art Ginsburg
Mr. Food®

WILLIAM MORROW AND COMPANY, INC.
New York

Copyright © 1995 by Cogin, Inc.

Illustrations copyright © 1995 by Michael Mendelsohn

All rights reserved. No part of this book may be reproduced or utilized in any form or by any means, electronic or mechanical, including photocopying, recording, or by any information storage or retrieval system, without permission in writing from the Publisher. Inquiries should be addressed to Permissions Department, William Morrow and Company, Inc., 1350 Avenue of the Americas, New York, N.Y. 10019.

It is the policy of William Morrow and Company, Inc., and its imprints and affiliates, recognizing the importance of preserving what has been written, to print the books we publish on acid-free paper, and we exert our best efforts to that end.

Library of Congress Cataloging-in-Publication Data

Ginsburg, Art.
   Mr. Food®'s fun kitchen tips and shortcuts (and recipes, too!) / Art Ginsburg.
     p. cm.
   Includes index.
   ISBN 0-688-13710-5
   1. Cookery.   I. Title.   II. Title: Mr. Food®'s fun kitchen tips and shortcuts (and recipes, too!).
TX651.G56   1995
641.5—dc20   94-45566
                                                                                                CIP

Printed in the United States of America

First Edition

1 2 3 4 5 6 7 8 9 10

BOOK DESIGN BY MICHAEL MENDELSOHN/MM DESIGN 2000, INC.

Dedicated to
Dad—
My greatest influence

Acknowledgments

What a year this has been! We moved the whole **MR. FOOD**® team into a new home in South Florida, where we can really spread out and have more space to do our "thing"—which is cooking, cooking, and more cooking for my television shows and cookbooks!

The move and this book couldn't have happened without the constant support and incredible perseverance of my family and colleagues. Each of them played a vital part in making it all come together, and I'm extremely grateful to them all.

Once again, I must thank Howard Rosenthal, a man of incredible energy and endless creativity. This book would not have been possible without Howard's input, or without the skillful eye of my daughter, Caryl Ginsburg Gershman. She continually pulls together my words and coordinates the creation of my books as "Art"-fully as only she can. My son, Steve Ginsburg, continues to lend all of us his experienced eye, and thanks to the creative input and computer wizardry of Roy Fantel, it was easier than ever to bring together all of this information.

Patty Rosenthal, Alice Palombo, and Monique Drummond have stepped into their new recipe testing roles masterfully, and none of us would have gotten this far without the caring, attentive assistance of Marilyn Ruderman, Beth Ives, and Stacey Dempsey.

I wouldn't miss another opportunity to thank my agent, Bill Adler, and my ever-energetic publicist, Phyllis Heller. To my

Acknowledgments

editor, Harriet Bell, and also to Al Marchioni, Skip Dye, Deborah Weiss Geline, and Kathleen Hackett at William Morrow, I extend more thanks for top-notch work.

As I said before, the "thank you mat" is out for Ethel, Chuck, and the rest of our growing family who are always there to give me the boosts I need. I really appreciate you guys.

My appreciation extends to the following companies and organizations, too, for their assistance in providing helpful information and product suggestions:

    American Spice Trade Association
    Goodness Gardens
    Kansas Meat Board
    Pillsbury
    Whirlpool

Contents

Acknowledgments
vii

Introduction
xi

Notes from MR. FOOD®
xiii

"You Wish You Knew This Before"
1

Kitchen Basics
40

Time and Money Savers
86

Better the Second Time Around
142

The Frills
172

Index
203

Introduction

Are you confused by the cover of this book? I guess it looks like I plan to pull a rabbit out of my hat and do fancy card tricks. Well, you know that's not what I usually do. But you also know that I *do* help you out with ideas for making magic of your own in the kitchen.

So, let's get started. I've gone through my bagful of kitchen tricks and come up with my all-time-best money-saving, time-saving tips that'll help you "magically" create dishes that'll disappear in no time!

I'll show you how to get dinner on the table quicker (page 90), make cleanup a snap—almost as fast as wiggling your nose (page 83)—and even how to make foods you thought were too tough to make at home, like Fast French Onion Soup (page 14), Blender Tomato Sauce (page 98), Cola Roast (page 116), Nutty Green Beans (page 188), and even Fruit Trifle (page 169) and Chocolate Sundae Sauce (page 182). I'll explain how to change stale bread into Crispy Croutons (page 153) and Quick Homemade Bread Crumbs (page 154)—and even how to make pickles without making your own brine . . . and they're ready in just one day (page 166)!

Did you think you had to be a wizard to make perfect hard-boiled eggs every time (page 4)? Can you imagine baking your favorite fruit bread or cake in about half the time it used to take (page 123)? Have you always wondered how most restaurants could make such light batters, but you couldn't (page 15)?

I've got those shortcuts and more! After all, isn't that what we all need today? We don't have lots of time to spend in the kitchen, but we still want to make fresh, homemade-tasting meals for ourselves and our families.

Introduction

Now, I know that magicians don't usually share their secrets, but I've decided that I have to share some of my best shortcut secrets with you . . . because we all need them more than ever! And after you try them, if you want to share them with your family and friends, just remember to build them up first with a little mystery.

Okay, get ready to become a kitchen magician and wow them without a wand. You're sure to leave them with an "Abracadabra!" *and* an "**OOH it's so GOOD!!**™"

Notes from MR. FOOD®

Lighten Up... with Cooking Sprays

Throughout this book, and in my other cookbooks, I frequently mention nonstick vegetable cooking spray and recommend using it to coat cookware and bakeware before placing food in or on them. Here's why—these sprays are easy to use, they add no measurable amount of fat to our food, and now they're even available in nonaerosol *and* in flavored varieties! The flavored sprays are super ways to add a touch of taste, either before or after cooking foods, without adding fat and calories. So far I've tried butter, olive oil, garlic, mesquite, and Oriental flavors. I think they do a great job of "greasing" *without* the grease.

Serving Sizes

I like to serve generous-sized portions myself, so I generally figure that way when I list the number of portions to expect from my recipes. That way you can have a good idea of how many people you can expect to serve with each dish. Yes, appetites do vary and *you* know the special food loves of your eaters, so, as always, you be the judge of how much to make.

Notes from Mr. Food

Packaged Foods

Packaged food sizes may vary by brand. Generally, the sizes indicated in these recipes are average sizes. If you can't find the exact package size listed in the ingredients, whatever package is closest in size will usually do the trick.

"You Wish You Knew This Before"

How many times have you struggled through a recipe, trying to figure out how to get part of it to work, or maybe struggling with an ingredient that isn't quite the way you need it to be?

That's happened to most of us. And if we ever figure it out, we end up saying, "Gee, I wish I knew that before!!"

That's what this chapter is all about. From the secret of how to make the perfect hard-boiled eggs (page 4) to making light batters (page 15) and getting the most juice from your lemons and other citrus (page 23), it's a bunch of answers to those problems that really bug us all at some time!

Most of our kitchen mysteries have really simple solutions. I use these tips all the time, so these shortcuts and tricks are sure to come in handy time after time in *your* kitchen, too.

Contents

"You Wish You Knew This Before"

How to Make Perfect Hard-Boiled Eggs (Finally!)	4
Recipe: Perfect Egg Salad	5
How to Soften Brown Sugar	6
Recipe: Bananas Foster	7
Frozen Tomato Paste Cubes	8
Recipe: Quick Chicken Tomato Soup	10
How to Test Baking Powder and Baking Soda for Freshness	11
Recipe: Mom's Baking Powder Biscuits	12
Peeling Onions with Fewer Tears	13
Recipe: Fast French Onion Soup	14
Making Light Batters	15
Recipe: Oriental Chicken Strips	16
Tips for Working with Oil	17

"You Wish You Knew This Before"

Bread Your Food, Not Your Fingers	20
Recipe: Friday Night Fried Fish	22
Getting the Most from Your Lemons	23
Recipe: Lemony Tartar Sauce	25
Fun Ways to Disguise Veggies	26
Recipe: Zucchini Cookies	28
Tips for Making Great Chicken Soup	29
Recipe: Mom's Chicken Soup	31
How to Tell Cooked Eggs from Raw Ones	32
Recipe: Perfect Deviled Eggs	33
How to Handle Hot Peppers Safely	34
Recipe: Fresh Chunky Tex-Mex Salsa	36
Lower-Fat Baking Tips	37
Recipe: Lower-Fat Brown Sugar Brownies	39

How to Make Perfect Hard-Boiled Eggs (Finally!)

Problem: I've always loved egg salad. When I was a kid I thought my mom made the absolute best egg salad—bright yellow and really tasty. Well, the first time I had egg salad at a friend's house, I was really confused. He *said* it was egg salad, and it tasted okay, but it looked funny. It was, well, "greenish." When I got home and asked my mom about it, she told me **if hard-boiled eggs are cooked too long, the yolks turn green.** That was a lesson I've always remembered! **So, what's the right way to hard-boil eggs?**

"Egg-xactly" Perfect Every Time

Here's how: Place the eggs in a large saucepan and add enough water to cover the eggs. Heat to boiling. When the water is boiling, remove the pan from the heat, cover, and let sit for 20 minutes (23 minutes for extra large or jumbo eggs). Drain the hot water and run cold water over the eggs. Add some ice cubes to the water and let the eggs cool for 5 to 10 minutes before peeling. That's it!

Perfect Egg Salad

4 servings

6 hard-boiled eggs, peeled
½ cup chopped celery
¼ cup chopped onion (optional)
1½ teaspoons prepared yellow mustard
¼ cup mayonnaise
¼ teaspoon salt
⅛ teaspoon pepper

In a medium-sized bowl, chop or mash the eggs to desired consistency with a fork. Mix in the remaining ingredients and stir until well combined.

NOTE: You can try lots of interesting add-ins, like chopped olives, sliced mushrooms, chopped red and green bell peppers (they're so colorful!), crushed potato chips, canned French-fried onions, even some tuna fish (one of my favorites!), cooked pasta (it gives you something to bite into), or for those really special times, maybe a bit of caviar on top!

How to Soften Brown Sugar

Problem: Your family has been after you for weeks to make those oatmeal-raisin cookies that melt in your mouth. So you finally put everything else aside and decide to make them. You get out all your ingredients and then **you find your box or bag of brown sugar and it's as hard as a rock!** You don't want to throw it out, so you wonder if there's any way you can soften it.

No More Brown Sugar Blues

Yup, if brown sugar is exposed to air, or if it sits in your cupboard for too long, it'll dry out and harden, so you should **always store it in an airtight container.** If it's too late, and yours has already hardened, here are a few tips to return it to its original texture:

- Place the sugar in an airtight container, with a wedge or two of fresh apple on top. Cover it tightly and allow to sit overnight. The next day, simply break up the softened sugar (with your hand or a spoon) and discard the apple.
- If you're in a hurry to use the brown sugar, place a few hard sugar pieces in a food processor with a cutting blade (or in a blender) and process on medium speed for several seconds. Remove this to a bowl and repeat with any remaining hardened sugar until all of it is returned to its original consistency.
- When it comes to brown sugar, most recipes call for it to be measured "firmly packed." This means exactly that—it must be firmly packed into the measuring cup, because if it isn't, it won't be a true measure of the amount needed in the recipe.

Bananas Foster

4 to 6 servings

Brown sugar and butter caramelized together make this New Orleans classic a real winner. It's "hoo hoo fancy" with so little work! Now, that's my kind of dessert!

¼ cup (½ stick) butter
½ cup firmly packed brown sugar
3 medium-sized bananas, sliced
⅓ cup light or dark rum
1 quart vanilla ice cream

In a medium-sized saucepan, melt the butter over medium heat. Then add the brown sugar and stir until a thick syrup forms. Add the sliced bananas and stir to coat evenly. Remove from the heat and stir in the rum. Place scoops of ice cream into 4 to 6 bowls or parfait glasses, and top with the banana mixture. Serve immediately.

Frozen Tomato Paste Cubes

Problem: How many times have **you needed just a little tomato paste and opened a whole can, only to realize you didn't have any use for the rest of the can?**

Square Tomatoes?!

Open a 12-ounce can of tomato paste (usually better value than the smaller cans, anyway) and **place a heaping tablespoon of paste into each compartment of a 12-compartment ice cube tray. Simply freeze overnight or until solid, then pop out the cubes and store in a sealed plastic bag.** Ready! The next time you need just a tablespoon or two of tomato paste . . . out come the frozen cubes and you've got what you need—and with no waste!

Here are some uses for those handy cubes that you may not have thought of:

- Why not add 1 or 2 cubes to jarred spaghetti sauce to give it a richer, thicker texture?
- Maybe add a tomato paste cube to canned tomato soup to give it that homemade taste. Then you may want to add an additional ¼ cup of milk or water to thin it a bit. Make adjustments to get the consistency you like.

Making the cubes is an almost no-fail way to have to-

"You Wish You Knew This Before"

mato paste on hand at all times—but just in case you run out, here are a few substitutes for tomato paste:
- Add ½ cup tomato sauce to a recipe in place of 1 tablespoon of tomato paste, and reduce the liquid in the recipe by ¼ cup.
- One tablespoon of ketchup is equal to 1 tablespoon of tomato paste. Ketchup isn't as concentrated, but it'll do the trick in a pinch.

Quick Chicken Tomato Soup

4 to 6 servings

Here's a quick way to enjoy some of those tomato paste cubes...

2 cans (10½ ounces each) condensed chicken broth
2 chicken broth cans of water
2 tablespoons tomato paste (2 frozen cubes right from the freezer are perfect!)
¾ cup small carrot chunks (2 to 3 carrots)
½ cup coarsely chopped onion (1 small onion)
¼ teaspoon dried basil
½ cup uncooked long-grain or whole-grain rice

Combine all the ingredients, except the rice, in a large saucepan over high heat. Bring to a boil, then reduce the heat to low and add the rice. Simmer for 30 to 35 minutes, or until the rice and vegetables are tender.

How to Test Baking Powder and Baking Soda for Freshness

Problem: **What could be worse than flat, hard baking powder biscuits** when you're expecting to bite into light, moist treats? It happened to my cousin recently—even with my mom's recipe! She couldn't figure out what went wrong until I told her that maybe **her baking powder was no longer "activated."** She asked me how you would know that, and this is the answer.

Does Your Baking Powder Still Pack a Punch?

This is how to make sure you'll be successful with baking powder baked goods:

- If you have any doubts about the freshness of your baking powder, **test it to see if it's still active.** Place 1 tablespoon water in a small bowl and add ¼ teaspoon of your baking powder. If it bubbles and fizzes, it's still good as new. If it's flat and there's no reaction, then it's stale and won't work the way it's supposed to in your recipes. If stored tightly covered, and away from heat at room temperature, baking powder should last for 12 to 18 months after the container has been opened.
- A similar test also works to test the freshness of baking soda. Just add ¼ teaspoon baking soda to 1 tablespoon white vinegar. If it bubbles and fizzes, you're all set.
- What to do if your baking soda *is* stale? Pour it down your kitchen drain to help eliminate odors and freshen up your pipes and garbage disposal.

Mom's Baking Powder Biscuits

16 to 18 biscuits

Try these surefire biscuits once you know my secret for getting perfect results every time. Yes, it really is all in the baking powder!

½ cup vegetable shortening, plus extra for greasing cookie sheets
2 cups all-purpose flour, plus extra for topping biscuits and for coating cookie sheets
1 teaspoon salt
4 teaspoons baking powder
¼ cup sugar
1 cup milk
1 teaspoon vanilla extract

Preheat the oven to 425°F. Grease and flour 2 large cookie sheets. In a large bowl, combine the 2 cups flour, salt, baking powder, and sugar. Sift the mixture into a medium-sized bowl. (No, it's not absolutely necessary to sift it, but sifting it does give better results.) Add the ½ cup shortening and, with your fingertips, combine the ingredients until the mixture has the appearance of fine crumbs. In a small bowl, combine the milk and vanilla; add to the flour mixture, stirring until well mixed. Scoop the dough by tablespoonfuls and drop onto the prepared cookie sheets, leaving about ½ inch between the biscuits. Dust the tops with flour and bake for 15 to 18 minutes, until golden. Serve hot.

NOTE: Serve plain or with butter at dinner, or maybe with jam at breakfast. And why not serve these with fresh or thawed frozen fruit and whipped cream as a special treat?! WOW!!

Peeling Onions with Fewer Tears

Problem: You wouldn't believe how many stories I've heard for **preventing tears when cutting onions. Do any of them really work?**

Onion Fears? No More Tears!

Okay, I'm going to pass along some of the more reasonable suggestions I've tried. All of them work at least sometimes, but none of them works every time for everybody. I recommend trying these and seeing which one works best for you:

- Peel onions under cold running water.
- Cut off the root end of the onion *last*. By cutting off the root ends last, you release less onion juice while you're cutting, producing less of the vapor that makes you cry (at least until the end, that is!).
- Turn on your kitchen exhaust fan or use a fan to blow the onion "vapor" away from you.
- Minimize your cutting time by using a food processor or blender to chop onions.
- Even though uncut onions shouldn't be stored in the refrigerator, a cold onion is less likely to make you cry than one at room temperature—so maybe keep 1 or 2 in the refrigerator ready for cutting, and replace them as you use them.

ONION TIP: You can rid your hands of onion odor by rubbing them with a mixture of lemon juice and salt. (Watch out if you have any cuts on your hands!)

Fast French Onion Soup

about 8 servings

Once you find a way to cut down on your onion tears, you'll have no problem mixing up a batch of your own onion soup. Would you invite me over?

- 2 tablespoons vegetable oil
- 2 medium-sized onions, peeled and cut into ¼"-thick slices
- 3 cans (14½ ounces each) beef broth
- 2 cups water
- ¼ teaspoon black pepper
- ⅓ cup dry red wine
- ¼ cup grated Parmesan cheese

In a medium-sized skillet, heat the oil over medium-high heat. Sauté the onions for 10 to 15 minutes, until browned. Place the onions in a large saucepan and combine with the beef broth, water, and pepper. Reduce the heat to low and simmer for about 20 minutes. Mix in the wine and cheese and continue cooking over low heat until mixed through. Serve immediately or keep warm until ready to serve.

NOTE: Serve topped with a few homemade croutons (page 153) and your family won't be able to say anything but "Ooh-la-la!"

Making Light Batters

Problem: So many people I talk to around the country ask me how to make light batters, like the ones we all get in restaurants. **They tell me they've tried everything and still end up with batters as heavy as cement!**

Some Like 'Em Light

Here we go! Forget about those past failures and try this trick for making batter so light that you'll practically need two hands to keep it from floating away! **It's all in adding fresh club soda to the batter.** The carbonation gets trapped inside the mixture, so that extra air means lighter finished dishes. Simply replace the liquid called for in the ingredients with the same amount of club soda—or almost any carbonated beverage. Club soda has the most fizz and tastes like water when mixed in. But if you'd like a fresh citrus taste, use a lemon-lime–flavored seltzer or soda. Just make sure that whatever flavor beverage you use goes with the rest of the ingredients! And, of course, there are no other rules. Try this with all of your batters.

- Add club soda or orange soda to pancake batter to make light pancakes every time. (Orange-flavored soda will make orange-flavored pancakes—the kids will love 'em!)
- Try replacing some of the liquid in your favorite cookie or cake recipes with a bit of club soda. WOW! What light and fluffy desserts you'll have!
- And if you've got any club soda that's gone flat? Use it in your house plants and watch how they perk up!

Oriental Chicken Strips

4 to 5 servings

Wait till you see how easily these chicken "bites" go down! They're so light!

- 3 whole boneless and skinless chicken breasts, each sliced lengthwise into 8 strips
- ½ cup teriyaki sauce
- 2 cups pancake mix
- 3 tablespoons sesame seed
- 4½ teaspoons paprika
- ½ teaspoon black pepper
- 1½ cups club soda
- 1 cup vegetable oil

Place the chicken strips and the teriyaki sauce in a medium-sized bowl. Completely cover the chicken with the sauce and allow the chicken to marinate for 10 minutes. Place the pancake mix in a large bowl. Add the sesame seed, paprika, and pepper. Add the club soda and mix well. Shake any excess liquid off the chicken, then dip it in the batter. Heat the oil in a large skillet over medium-high heat. Test the oil to see if it is ready (see below). Fry the battered chicken strips until golden on both sides. Drain on paper towels and serve immediately.

NOTE: If these need to be reheated, place them on a baking pan that has been coated with nonstick vegetable spray. Bake at 350°F. for about 15 minutes or until hot and crispy.

HOW TO TEST THE OIL: Add a little of the batter to the oil. If it bubbles lightly and turns golden brown, it's ready. If the batter floats to the bottom, it's not ready. If it burns quickly, remove the skillet from the heat and wait for the oil to cool. Then return it to the heat and test it again before adding the chicken strips.

Tips for Working with Oil

Problem: We all love the taste of fried foods. Sure, even if we want to limit the amount of fried foods we eat, it's still hard to resist a batch of fresh French fries or a crispy, warm apple fritter. Oh, boy—just thinking about 'em makes me hungry! **So many people want to make special fried foods at home but don't really know how to do it. I'll tell you!**

Fried Food Frenzy

You don't have to have an industrial kitchen to fry foods properly. Today there are a number of portable deep fryers available for those of us who do lots of frying. No, they're not essential, but they're the ideal way to fry because they have thermostats that keep the oil at a desired temperature. That's the trick to deep frying—the oil must be fresh and at the correct temperature. The temperature should remain as close to constant as possible. Here are a few hints to help you with your frying:

- If you don't have a deep fryer, you can certainly panfry lots of things in a thin layer of oil. And if you want to make foods that require deep frying, I recommend using a large soup pot filled no more than ⅓ full with vegetable oil.
- Use a probe-type food or candy thermometer to keep an eye on the oil temperature. The desired temperature may vary, depending on the items being fried. The range is usually be-

continued

tween 300°F. and 450°F. Generally, you should fry larger items, such as fried chicken and veal cutlets, at lower temperatures and smaller items, such as French fries and Onion Strings (page 73), at higher temperatures.

- If you don't have a thermometer, test the oil by dropping a cube of bread into the hot oil. After 1 minute, if the bread is golden brown, then the oil is ready. If it's soaked with oil and stays a pale color, then the oil is not hot enough. If the bread has burned, the oil is too hot; turn off the heat immediately until it cools down. Then reheat the oil and try again.
- Add only a few items at a time to hot oil. Too many items added at once will cool down the oil and make the food taste greasy.
- If you are frying a lot of food, it may be necessary to add some additional oil, a little at a time, in order to keep the oil at its original level in the pan.
- **Always use caution when working with and around hot oil!**
- Use a large pair of tongs or a long-handled fork or spoon to place items into and remove them from hot oil.
- Remember to keep the handles of all pots, especially those containing oil, turned so that they do not get bumped. It's important to keep the oil from splattering and spilling.
- If oil is left unattended over the heat, it will eventually reach beyond a smoke point and will burst into flames. If a fire should begin, quickly and carefully place a pan lid on top of the pan. This should smother the fire. **Do not pour water onto a grease fire. Water will only make it spread!**
- A small pan fire can be extinguished by removing the pan from the burner and pouring baking soda or salt on the grease. It is also recommended to have a fire extinguisher

"You Wish You Knew This Before"

available in your kitchen. They come in different types for handling different types of fires. (They're even available now in lots of sizes, shapes, and colors.) Check with your local hardware store or fire extinguisher supplier to see which type is best for your particular needs.
- Do not pour used oil down the drain! Let it cool, then pour it into a nonrecyclable container, cover tightly, and dispose of with other garbage.

If patience and care are maintained, frying can be safe and give you results that you used to think were available only in restaurants!

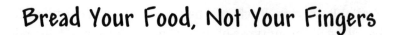

Bread Your Food, Not Your Fingers

Problem: When I used to make fried chicken or fish or, well, really anything breaded, **I always ended up with more breading on my fingers than I did on the food that was supposed to be breaded.** Not anymore! There's a solution to this messy task that'll make everybody say, "Of course!"

No More Sticky Fingers

This hint is for all the cooks out there with clumps of breading stuck on their fingertips. Here's the trick: **Keep one hand dry and one hand wet!** Sounds easy, but it does take a little practice. It goes like this: Let's say your recipe calls for dipping fish into flour, then egg, then seasoned bread crumbs. Use your left hand to put the wet fish into the flour, without touching the flour. Next, use your right hand to pat the flour gently onto the fish. Next, with your right hand, put the fish into the eggs. With your wet left hand, remove the fish to the bread crumbs, and bread the fish with your dry right hand. That's it! No magic, no fancy utensils, just easy breading every time.

Here are a few more tips to make you a breading pro:
- You can use egg mixed with milk instead of plain egg, or just milk alone. Milk doesn't have as much "sticking power" as egg, but it works, and it's lower in fat.

"You Wish You Knew This Before"

- Before placing food to be breaded in flour, use paper towels to pat it dry.
- Try placing bread crumbs in a resealable plastic bag and shaking the final breading onto your foods.
- Be sure to test the oil to see if it is ready for frying. How to do that? See my tips on pages 17 to 19.

Friday Night Fried Fish

4 servings

Here's a great recipe for the next time you want to coat and fry fish (not fingers!).

1 cup all-purpose flour
3 eggs, beaten
2 cups plain bread crumbs
½ teaspoon garlic powder
½ teaspoon dried oregano
1½ pounds white-fleshed fish, such as haddock, cod, or whiting, cut into 4-ounce fillets
1 cup vegetable oil

Place the flour, eggs, and bread crumbs in three separate pie plates. Combine the garlic powder and oregano with the bread crumbs. Rinse the fish with cold water and pat dry with a paper towel. Dip the fillets, one at a time, into the flour with one hand, then dip the floured fish into the beaten eggs with the other hand. Use your dry hand to coat the fish with the bread crumbs. Place the breaded fish on a plate. When all the fish has been breaded, heat the oil in a large skillet over medium-high heat. Fry the fish until brown on both sides. Remove from the skillet and drain on paper towels.

NOTE: Why not serve this with my quick Lemony Tartar Sauce (page 25)?

Getting the Most from Your Lemons

Problem: For years I wondered if there was any way to squeeze more juice out of my fresh lemons. **I always had to squeeze and squeeze to get just a little bit of juice.** Sure, it tasted right-from-the-tree fresh, but trying to squeeze out every tablespoon of juice was a chore.

"The Big Squeeze"

Now, let's juice! First, try to choose large lemons. Then place the lemons on your kitchen counter or table and roll them around while gently but firmly pressing down on them with the palm of your hand. The lemons will begin to soften. Next, place them in the microwave (if you have one) and heat them on high power for 10 to 15 seconds. Next, cut the lemons in half and squeeze gently. Wait till you see how much more juice you'll get! And it saves your hands from all that squeezing and your pocketbook from wasting all that juice that you could never get out before! If you don't have a microwave oven, don't worry. Just place the lemons in a bowl of warm water for 5 minutes.

Yes, this works with any citrus. Hooray! And here are some fresh citrus tips:
- Squeeze fresh lemon juice over vegetable salads and cooked veggies.

continued

"You Wish You Knew This Before"

- Grate the citrus peel and add it to your favorite cake mixes. The "zest" will give your cakes a whole new dimension.
- Add the empty citrus shells to lemonade or orange juice for a fresh taste twist.
- Cut the remaining shells into small pieces and put them down the garbage disposal to freshen it up.

Lemony Tartar Sauce

1 ¼ cups

Why squeeze fresh lemon on your fish and then dip it into tartar sauce? This recipe puts the two together with one big taste!

1 cup mayonnaise
3 tablespoons pickle relish, drained
1 tablespoon chopped scallions
4 teaspoons fresh lemon juice

In a small bowl, combine all the ingredients and mix well. Chill until ready to serve.

NOTE: This will last for 2 to 3 weeks in the refrigerator if covered tightly—so go ahead and make a double batch!

Fun Ways to Disguise Veggies

Problem: I like sweets, but I also love my veggies. Many people, no matter what age, never have a problem making room for cookies and desserts, but when it comes to vegetables . . . that's a different story! **I think some people shy away from them because they just aren't familiar with them or aren't used to including them in their regular eating.** So, how can we painlessly eat more veggies?

It's in There . . . !

I figured out a way to get some healthy foods like carrots and zucchini into everyone's favorite foods. Most of us know how awesome carrots taste in carrot cake . . . so maybe the sweet-eaters will admit that carrots aren't really that bad!

How 'bout trying a few of these combinations or ideas to see if you can have those same sweet-eaters eating healthier in every part of the meal (even with cookie jar treats!):

- Toss some shredded vegetables into ground meat when making meat loaf.
- Add some shredded carrots, zucchini, or other veggies to spaghetti sauce or other favorite dishes. You can even add them to pasta to make your own Pasta Primavera.
- Pizza is a great way to introduce veggies to children. After all, what kid of any age doesn't go for pizza?! And exciting new toppings are really "in" these days, too. (Why, just look at all the gourmet pizza shops springing up around the coun-

"You Wish You Knew This Before"

try!) See page 131 for my Quick and Easy Pizza. Making it at home is a great way to introduce your gang to new veggies. (And at the beginning they might not even notice them if you hide them in the other toppings!)

- Make some fun by adding a selection of veggies to chicken noodle soup. If you add peas and thinly sliced carrots, you can tell the kids that they're eating all the Os and Hs from lots of "OOH it's so GOOD!!™"

Zucchini Cookies

about 4 dozen cookies

Here's the ultimate trick for getting them to eat their veggies... but let's keep the special ingredient our secret!

½ cup (1 stick) butter, softened
1 cup sugar
1 egg, beaten
2 cups all-purpose flour
1 teaspoon baking soda
1 teaspoon ground cinnamon
½ teaspoon salt
1 cup grated zucchini (about 1 small zucchini)
1 cup raisins
1 cup chopped walnuts
1 cup (1 6-ounce package) semisweet chocolate chips

Preheat the oven to 350°F. In a large bowl, cream together the butter and sugar until light and fluffy. Gradually add the egg, flour, baking soda, cinnamon, and salt; mix well. Stir in the zucchini, raisins, walnuts, and chocolate chips. Drop by teaspoonfuls onto cookie sheets that have been coated with nonstick vegetable spray. Bake for 15 to 20 minutes or until golden. Do not overbake.

Tips for Making Great Chicken Soup

Problem: I grew up on chicken soup. When we were sick *and* when we weren't, my mom often had a big pot of it simmering away on the stovetop. What a small—what a flavor! **You say you don't make homemade chicken soup because it's too much bother?** It's really not! There's something about chicken soup that makes you feel so cozy, so healthy, and brings back lots of warm memories. Don't miss out! Make yourself some soon.

Mom's "Souper" Cold Medicine

I've heard lots of theories about why chicken soup is the best medicine for the common cold. Some say it's because it brings back fond memories of Mom, while others insist that the heat of the soup helps break up congestion, giving some quick relief from the cold. But now there is research that has doctors believing that there really *is* something medicinal in chicken soup.

The options for what can go into your chicken soup are as endless as the search for the cure for the common cold! The Jewish version comes with matzo balls and the Oriental version has won tons, while German-style chicken soup usually comes with spaetzle. Today's newer versions are made with anything from hot pepper sauce for some zing to the very fancy lemongrass.

continued

Here are a few basic tips for making "Jewish Penicillin":

- Use the whole chicken (wings, gizzards, breasts, and bones) except the liver, because it discolors the soup.
- If you're planning to eat the chicken, then don't boil it for more than two hours or the chicken meat will get mushy and lose all its flavor.
- Add as wide a variety of vegetables as possible. They add flavor and nutrients.
- You may want to add a bit of bouillon or maybe some instant soup mix right before serving. No, it's not cheating, it just gives the soup an extra flavor boost.
- After finishing the soup, let it cool slightly, then cover and refrigerate it overnight. The next day, the fat will have risen to the top and solidified. Just scoop it off and discard it to cut down on the oily, fatty taste. Or, if you want to serve it right away, stir about 6 ice cubes into the warm soup for about 30 seconds. Remove the cubes before they melt—the fat should stick to them!

Mom's Chicken Soup

8 to 10 servings

Here's a real comfort food, a pick-me-up when you're sick and even when you're not!

1 chicken (3 to 4 pounds), cut into 8 pieces
4 quarts cold water
3 to 4 carrots, peeled and cut into chunks
2 to 3 celery stalks, cut into chunks
2 medium-sized onions, cut into chunks
Salt to taste
Pepper to taste

Rinse the chicken under cold running water. Place all the ingredients in a soup pot and bring to a boil. Reduce the heat, cover, and simmer for 2 to 3 hours, or until the chicken meat falls off the bones, stirring occasionally. Serve immediately or store as directed on the previous page.

NOTE: You can adjust the cooking time according to how much chicken flavor you want the soup to have—I like to wait until the meat falls off the bones. Here are some variations I like, too:

- Strain the soup for a clear broth or serve it with just the veggies in it (reserving the chicken to make a great salad).
- Use white pepper instead of black so there are no black specks.
- Use different amounts of any of the vegetables, and maybe include a few parsnips, too. They really sweeten it up.
- Add any or all of these: fresh dill, parsley, and garlic cloves.

How to Tell Cooked Eggs from Raw Ones

Problem: As I said before, my mom loved to make egg salad, and when she did she sometimes made a few extra hard-boiled eggs and left them on the refrigerator door. Sometimes she remembered to mark them with an "X," but when she forgot... total egg confusion! We never knew how to tell the raw eggs from the hard-boiled ones. **Let me tell you, it can be a pretty messy problem when you mistake a raw egg for a hard-boiled one!**

Taking Your Eggs for a Spin

It's really easy to tell cooked eggs from raw ones... just take them for a spin! **Place an egg on the counter and give it a gentle spin. If it spins easily and quickly, it's hard-boiled; if it doesn't... yup, it's raw.** Things would have been so much easier if I had known this trick years ago! (It sure would've saved lots of guessing *and cleaning up!*)

Perfect Deviled Eggs

18 egg halves

A great breakfast, lunch, or dinner treat—even an ideal snack. And when they're done right, their bright yellow centers are so colorful!

9 eggs
¼ cup mayonnaise
1½ teaspoons prepared mustard
Pinch of salt
⅛ teaspoon pepper
1 teaspoon sweet relish, drained (optional)
¼ teaspoon paprika for sprinkling

Place the eggs in a large saucepan and add just enough water to cover them. Heat to boiling. When the water is boiling, remove the pan from the heat, cover, and let sit for 20 minutes (23 minutes for extra large or jumbo eggs). Drain the hot water and run cold water over the eggs. Add some ice cubes to the water and let the eggs cool for 5 to 10 minutes. Peel the eggs, slice in half lengthwise, and remove the egg yolks to a small bowl. Add the mayonnaise, mustard, salt, pepper, and relish. Mix well and fill the egg white halves with the yolk mixture. Sprinkle with paprika, cover lightly with plastic wrap, and refrigerate until ready to serve.

How to Handle Hot Peppers Safely

Problem: "Help!! I love the taste of fresh jalapeño peppers in my Tex-Mex cooking, but **whenever I clean the peppers, the juices and seeds sting my hands. Should I stop using fresh hot peppers, or is there a solution?**" In my travels I often get this question—and here's my answer.

Give Hot Peppers a Hand

Don't stop using hot peppers because of a little sting—unless, of course, it's advised by a doctor. I've found that if you **rub your hands well with vegetable oil before handling the peppers**, the oil acts like a pair of invisible gloves to protect you from the sting of the juices and seeds that would otherwise react with your unprotected skin. You must still be very careful not to rub your eyes or the corners of your mouth with your hands until you wash them well, because the pepper oil will sting your eyes and mouth, too! Coating your hands with oil like this will also help when:

- Peeling lots of carrots. The color from the carrots won't absorb as readily into the skin.
- Working with fish. The fish odor won't be as strong on the skin.

"You Wish You Knew This Before"

- Working with onions. If protected this way, your hands shouldn't pick up the smell of the onion juice as strongly. If the onion odor still remains afterward, rub your hands with some fresh lemon and salt—but try to keep the lemon out of any open cuts you may have on your hands!

IF YOU TRY THIS TIP, BE CAREFUL! COATING YOUR HANDS WITH OIL WILL MAKE THEM SLIPPERY, SO REMEMBER TO BE CAUTIOUS WHEN HANDLING A KNIFE OR OTHER KITCHEN UTENSILS.

Fresh Chunky Tex-Mex Salsa

about 1½ cups

Most of us know that jalapeño peppers taste hot. But did you know that if you don't handle them carefully, the oils in the peppers could irritate your skin? Be sure to try my tip on page 34, because their heat and special flavor add so much to our favorite foods that they're worth the extra effort.

1 can (14½ ounces) stewed tomatoes, drained and chopped
¼ cup minced onion
¼ cup diced green bell pepper
1 jalapeño pepper, seeded and minced
½ teaspoon garlic powder
½ teaspoon white vinegar
⅛ teaspoon cayenne pepper

Combine all the ingredients in a small bowl. Refrigerate for 1 hour or overnight.

NOTE: For medium salsa, add an extra ⅛ teaspoon cayenne pepper. For hot salsa, add an extra ¼ teaspoon.

This sauce is like all your favorites in one! Here are some serving suggestions:
- Use as a dip with tortilla chips or crackers.
- This is the perfect sauce if you want to make pizza with pizzazz!
- It's a great topping for hamburgers and hot dogs.
- Combine equal parts of salsa and spaghetti sauce and serve over your favorite cooked pasta. Watch your family come back for seconds and thirds!

Lower-Fat Baking Tips

Problem: Are you one of the many people who think that low-fat means no taste? Well, it's not true! Sure, there are lots of items out there that claim to be lower in fat or the absolute answer to good health. Well, I know of no one product that can do everything! But, **how can we do what's best for our bodies while still enjoying what we eat (without a lot of work)?**

Low Fat, High Taste

Sure, eating lower-fat foods is an issue for many of us, but that doesn't mean we have to go crazy about it. My suggestion is to **use moderation!** Unless otherwise directed by your physician, you can simply cut back on a little of this and a little of that. Instead of having a 10-ounce main dish portion, maybe have a 7-ounce portion—and this way you don't feel like you're being denied. Of course, before we go for that second piece of cake, we should remember that 1 piece of cake has half the fat and calories of 2 pieces of cake. (Right? Of course, right!) Without sacrificing taste, there are ways we can alter our cooking habits by changing a few basics. Try these:

- When baking cookies or cakes, use applesauce in a direct one-to-one substitution for vegetable oil or butter. And you can also use prune purée in the same one-to-one substitution in darker baked goods. You'll be surprised that the taste is so good *and* the fat is reduced. You should be able to find prune purée in the jam and jelly or baking section of your

continued

"You Wish You Knew This Before"

supermarket, or you can make your own by combining 1⅓ cups (8 ounces) pitted prunes and 6 tablespoons water in the container of a food processor. Pulse on and off until the mixture is smooth. It makes 1 cup.

- Try replacing whole eggs with either egg whites or with packaged egg substitutes (found in the refrigerator and freezer sections of the supermarket).
- Use fat-free or lower-fat versions of things like sour cream, cheese, cream cheese, and yogurt.
- Many manufacturers are now offering reduced-fat or no-fat versions of their products. However, this doesn't necessarily mean that they're also lower in everything else! If you're watching calories and other things, you still need to be cautious. **Always consult your physician for your specific dietary guidelines.** And if these new products fit your lifestyle and diet, give them a try!

Lower-Fat Brown Sugar Brownies

12 to 16 brownies

Less fat doesn't have to mean less taste. Here's the proof! This recipe uses applesauce in place of butter—and is it ever a flavor-packed winner! Make these blond brownies and see if your family knows the difference.

½ cup unsweetened applesauce
2 cups firmly packed dark brown sugar
2 eggs, well beaten (see Note)
1 cup all-purpose flour
1 teaspoon baking powder
1 teaspoon vanilla extract
1 cup pecan pieces (see Note)
Confectioners' sugar for sprinkling (optional)

Preheat the oven to 350°F. In a large bowl, combine the applesauce, brown sugar, and eggs; mix thoroughly. Add the flour and baking powder and blend. Stir in the vanilla and nuts. Pour the mixture into a well-greased 8-inch square baking pan and bake for 35 to 40 minutes. Cool in the pan, then cut into squares and sprinkle with confectioners' sugar, if desired.

NOTE: To reduce the fat even more, you can use an egg substitute. And instead of pecans, use the same amount of granola.

Kitchen Basics

Stop! Before you spend another minute in the kitchen, you've got to read this chapter. No, there won't be a quiz, and, as a matter of fact, I think you'll even enjoy reading this information, because you'll get some hints on how to organize your kitchen (and we can all use some help with that!—so see page 47), store spices (page 55) and foods (page 61), and even tips to help cut down on your shopping time (page 43).

I've also included suggestions for different ways to use some of your everyday kitchen equipment (page 80) and ideas for keeping your refrigerator clean and uncluttered (page 53).

This chapter has some really great *easy* recipes, but it's mostly full of information that should be helpful for everyone who works in the kitchen, from beginner to old hand. So, before you move on, have some fun with these tips. They're just more simple ways to help you put a little **MR. FOOD**® magic into your kitchen.

Contents

Kitchen Basics

Grocery Shopping Tips	43
Tips for Organizing Your Kitchen	47
Tips on Purchasing and Caring for Knives	50
Tips for Keeping Your Refrigerator Clean and Uncluttered	53
Easy Ways to Spice Up Your Foods	55
Food Storage Tips	61
Measuring Up: A Guide to Easy Food Measurement	65
How to Get the Most Kitchen Help from Aluminum Foil	67
Recipe: Wrapped-Up Cornish Hens	69
Creating Your Own Cookie Cutters	70
Recipe: Sugar Cookies	71

Tips for Storing Fresh Onions	72
Recipe: Onion Strings	**73**
How to Bone a Chicken Breast	74
Recipe: Russian Chicken	**77**
Storage Time for Leftovers	78
Using Everyday Kitchen Items in All-New Ways	80
Recipe: Cookie Cups	**82**
Easy Tips for Keeping Your Kitchen Clean	83

Grocery Shopping Tips

Problem: **Hate grocery shopping??** You're not alone! Yes, grocery shopping takes time. We have to check our fridge and cabinets, then make our lists, check for coupons, go to the store, choose our items, then unpack and put them away when we get home. But **it's something that's gotta be done—so how 'bout some tips to make it as easy and efficient as possible?**

Making a List and Checking It Twice

So many people have asked me for advice on how to save time and money at the store, so here's my "shopping cart" of tips:

- Make a list. Even if you're sure you know what you need, you'll do better if you make yourself a list. And if your gang is like mine and always has something to say about what you buy, then get them involved in making the list, too. That way they can have their say ahead of time *and* give you more of a chance to please everybody!
- Try to shop at off-peak hours. Peak hours are after work (just before dinner) and weekend mornings, so try to avoid those times. Instead, try early on weekday mornings, or in the evening. You'll save a bunch of time just by doing that. (And wouldn't you rather spend your shopping time picking the best tomatoes instead of picking the best route around all the other shopping carts?!)
- Is it best to shop on a full or empty stomach? Shopping experts disagree on this point. If you shop on an empty stom-

continued

Kitchen Basics

ach, you're more apt to buy on impulse. After all, it's no fun to go through the aisles with your stomach growling! And you may be in too much of a hurry to pick up everything you really need. But if you shop on a full stomach, things may not be as appealing to you, and you still may not get everything you need. (That's where the all-important list comes in really handy.) I know you can't always choose the best time to shop, so if you have to do it before a meal, I suggest having a light snack before you go.

- Clipping coupons does you no good if you forget to take them shopping with you! Have an organizer envelope or box to keep coupons together by product type so that you can save time and money—but only if they're for products that you're going to use. Remember to check coupon expiration dates in advance.
- Watch weekly store advertisements for the sales that usually begin on Thursdays. That's when the supplies of the special items are plentiful. Many of these on-sale items are considered "loss leaders" by the stores. That means that they reduce their prices on certain popular items to entice you into their store. Take advantage of these sales whenever possible, but don't get trapped into buying nonsale items that you know are overpriced on that same shopping trip.
- Check your list carefully as you shop, checking off items and making notes if you need to.
- Should you buy store brands instead of national brands? It's up to you. Store brands are usually priced better, and are often processed and packaged by the same companies that process and package the national brands. But you should always check the labels and compare the individual items.

Kitchen Basics

You won't get good value from a product if your family won't eat or use it!

- Don't forget to check the high and low shelves in the supermarket. Often the best bargains are there, not at eye level.
- Keep in mind the price difference between convenience foods and homemade foods. You're the specialist on what your family likes and what you have time for. Sometimes it ends up being less expensive to buy a bag of mixed salad greens instead of separate types of fresh greens.

Here's a list of other things to remember:

- Don't buy dented cans or any products with cracked seals.
- Check label dates. The dates listed are generally the last date that the food can be sold, and not the last date they can be eaten.
- Carefully check produce for bruises and soft spots. Hand-picking each of your items from the produce counters helps to ensure that you buy high-quality items. An example is oranges—if you buy a large bag of them, you can't examine each one like you can if you pick them out individually. Bulk packages are usually priced better, but if you end up buying items that you can't eat... there go your savings!
- Buy meat, poultry, and fish as fresh as possible, and be sure the item you choose is really what you want. Don't buy ground turkey if you really want ground beef, etc. Ask the butcher for suggestions. He's the pro and can probably save you some money.
- Don't buy frozen foods that look like they've been thawed and refrozen. Also, ask the checkout person to pack the frozen items in plastic bags or freezer bags so they won't thaw or make a mess before you get them home. It might be a

continued

Kitchen Basics

good idea to keep an inexpensive cooler in the car for getting these things home.
- Buy just enough baked goods for a few days. Don't buy a week's worth at a time because, chances are, they won't stay fresh. It's better to pick up select items throughout the week.

Tips for Organizing Your Kitchen

Problem: Is your kitchen a jumble of pots, pans, utensils, gadgets, appliances, and food? It's time to get organized!

Putting Pots and Pans in Their Place

A lot of my success in the kitchen comes from being organized. Now that doesn't mean that you can't be a good cook if you're not an organized person, but it sure makes things easier if you get organized *before* you start cooking. Let me give you a few pointers that will get you on the track to becoming a kitchen wizard:

- Organize pots and pans. Nest them inside each other to make more room in the cupboard. Put the ones you use just once in a while in the back, and the ones you use all the time in the front.
- Find a kitchen carousel or a tall wide-mouthed ceramic container for storing your most-used cooking utensils (except knives—see the next tip, as well as page 50 for more information on storing knives). It makes it much easier to find your utensils if they're right on the counter instead of jumbled up in a drawer.
- Get a knife rack or a knife magnet for storing knives. Keep them out of the flow of traffic but within easy reach. It can be dangerous reaching into a utensil drawer and getting stuck by a sharp knife!
- Organize your herbs and spices. Use a spice rack or organize them on a cabinet turntable. You can even put them in a shoebox . . . plastic ones (like the ones available at national

continued

Kitchen Basics

discount stores) work well. It makes sense to keep your herbs and spices together, because they're easier to find. Some people even alphabetize them so they can find them in a snap. (I've got more on herbs and spices on pages 55 to 60.)
- A paper towel holder is a must, because you need them handy but out of the way. There are lots of colors and types available now. Some hang and others stand alone on the counter, in materials from plastic to wood and even Lucite.
- Store your most-used packaged food items within easy reach, and store seldom-used foods on higher shelves. Try to keep foods of the same type together, like all canned goods, and also sugar, flour, and other baking supplies. Try to store foods in areas other than over the oven or refrigerator, because most packaged foods need to be kept in places that *don't* have extremes of hot or cold. Spices especially need to be stored in a cool place.
- Store taller items at the back of cabinets, so that you can easily see the shorter items in front. And try keeping odd-shaped items, like bags of pasta, in plastic storage containers. They stack more easily (and stay fresh longer, too).
- Keep the refrigerator clean! There are easy tips for doing that on page 53.
- Keep countertops uncluttered so that you have as much work space as possible. Store cookbooks neatly with bookends . . . maybe on top of the refrigerator or somewhere else out of the work area and safe from splatters and spills. Small appliances are best stored on a shelf. (Why work around your crockpot every day if you use it only once or twice a month?) There are even space-saving appliances available for helping you keep the most counter space available. (Don't forget to keep all electrical cords out of the way of water and heat!) And if, after doing all this, you still run out

Kitchen Basics

of counter space, just open your top utensil drawer halfway and place a cookie sheet or cutting board on top of it. There! More horizontal work space when we need it! (Just don't use it for chopping, or place anything very delicate *or* too heavy on it!)

- Keep plastic wrap, aluminum foil, and plastic bags organized in a drawer. You can also use a six-pack cardboard beverage holder as the perfect holder for standing up your boxes of wraps.
- A fire extinguisher is a kitchen must. Be sure to check with your local supplier and get one that covers all types of fires, including grease fires. And once you've got the right one for your purposes, be sure to store it in a handy place, not hidden in a cabinet or closet. Maybe hang it by an exit door. There are even colorful "designer" fire extinguishers, so they can blend in with any decor!

Tips on Purchasing and Caring for Knives

Problem: A bunch of couples had a get-together at a friend's house several weeks ago and we all pitched in and helped make the meal. Of course it was my job to do all the chopping and cutting of the vegetables. Well, I could have screamed because **every knife in the drawer was so dull!** There wasn't even a simple knife sharpener in the house! Boy, did it make me appreciate my own knives even more than I already did!

Getting to the Point

Knives are just about the most important kitchen items. No, they don't have to be expensive or imported. There are plenty of good ones around that are reasonably-priced. Here are a few tips to help you select and maintain these all-important kitchen tools:

- The chef's knife is the most versatile kitchen knife. It usually has a 6- to 10-inch blade, and the position of its handle allows for easy chopping and dicing. The blade is perfect for slicing meats, too!
- The paring knife is a handy tool because its 3- to 4-inch blade is perfect for smaller jobs like peeling apples, trimming potatoes, and slicing cheese.
- The bread slicer has an approximately 7-inch serrated blade (toothlike, like a saw blade) that makes it perfect for slicing bread, cake, or even some meat. Its blade is usually a bit more flexible than those of other types of knives.
- When selecting a knife, be certain that the handle is comfortable. Is it the perfect size for your hand? Does it have a

Kitchen Basics

safety guide to keep your hand from slipping onto the blade? Is the blade noncorrosive? If so, it'll be easier to clean and it should keep its sharp edge longer (provided it's well maintained).

- Knives should be washed and dried right after use. Never toss a knife into a sinkful of soapy water because someone might accidentally get cut by the blade. Also, soaking can harm knife handles. When drying knives, be sure to keep the sharp edges pointed away from fingers and bodies. Remember that a sharp knife can cut right through a towel.
- Knives should not be stored loose in a drawer. It's too easy to get cut that way. Put them in a holder like a butcher block or on a magnetic type of hanger. Even better is storing them with a plastic sheath over the blades. That way hands *and* blades are protected! A flattened empty cardboard paper towel tube will work well as a protective sheath.
- It's important that knives be kept sharp. There are many types of sharpeners available, and you don't need a fancy expensive one to get a sharp edge. It's good to have a sharpening steel to brush up a dull knife, but ask your kitchen supplier or hardware store to show you the best sharpener for your knives. There are manual, hand-held, tabletop, and electric types, and all of them work well if used properly. (Most serrated knives never require sharpening.) The most important advice I have for sharpening knives is to **BE CAREFUL.** A dull knife can cut you just as seriously as, if not worse than, a sharp one! (You could even ask your butcher to sharpen your knives. He might be happy you asked, and you'll be happy, too, 'cause your knives will be good as new!)
- Respect your knives and they should give you years of

continued

service. That means not using them as screwdrivers or for prying off the tops of cans. You could damage the points and bend the blades. Cut on plastic or wood cutting boards. Cutting on countertops will damage blades *and* countertops!

Tips for Keeping Your Refrigerator Clean and Uncluttered

Problem: Does your refrigerator look like a disaster area? Is it always a cluttered, disorganized mess? Does it smell funny?

Free Up the Fridge

If you expect to be able to work in your kitchen, then it's important to keep your refrigerator clean and full of fresh, usable food. Here are my suggestions for keeping it organized:

- Clean out the refrigerator before going grocery shopping. That way you'll know exactly what you've got on hand, while making room for new groceries. (And you can save money by not buying duplicates of things you forgot about that ended up stashed way in the back of the fridge!)
- Wrap leftovers well, then label and date them. It's as simple as using a marker and a piece of masking tape to eliminate the "Do you know what this is?" game later.
- Try to eat leftovers in a reasonable amount of time. Always toss out food that is too old to eat. Don't risk getting sick! (Check the chart on page 79 for some basic guidelines.)
- Don't use your fridge as a pantry. If something doesn't have to be kept cool, don't keep it in the fridge. Unopened maple syrup and open boxes of pancake mix don't belong in the fridge.
- Group like items together. Put all the jelly together, all the mustard together, and so on. They'll be easier to find.
- To keep your eggs fresh, alternate marking each batch

continued

Kitchen Basics

with an "X" or an "O" by marking the new ones after each shopping trip. That way you'll know which ones to use first—all the "X"s or all the "O"s. You could also alternate buying white and brown eggs—buy white eggs on one trip and brown the next. (Brown eggs are available in most areas and are the same as white—except for their shell color, of course!)

- Keep the seldom-used items in the back of the fridge. Why keep moving that almost-empty jar of hot fudge or pickles every time you need to get the milk?
- Place an open box of baking soda in the back of the fridge to absorb food odors. There are some pretty containers for holding baking soda in the fridge, and there are even some spill-proof boxes, too.
- If your freezer is not frost-free, defrost it often and regularly. (How often will vary by usage and model. Check your owner's manual.) If it is full of frost, this cuts down on usable inside space and it runs less efficiently. After defrosting and cleaning, try coating the inside freezer panels with nonstick vegetable spray to eliminate ice buildup; it'll mean easier defrosting and cleaning next time.
- Use your vegetable drawer and meat-saver compartments, if you have them. They really do prolong the shelf life of your food. Using them also frees up a lot of extra storage space.
- Keep your refrigerator clean, inside and out—and don't forget to clean the gaskets, too. Wipe up spills when they happen. Use a sponge with a little warm water mixed with a bit of baking soda to make cleanup a breeze.
- Make cleaning the refrigerator a rotating job for everyone in the family who's able. Yes, the kids can help, too. This way the whole family will respect your clean, uncluttered refrigerator and, hopefully, will help keep it that way!

Easy Ways to Spice Up Your Foods

Problem: Lots of us eat out because **so many of the foods we like just seem to taste better when somebody else makes them.** Well, sometimes there's a simple reason why: the flavorings. So many people are afraid to experiment with spices and herbs—but, except for food allergies or restrictions, there's no reason not to try some new ones. It's easy!

Add Spice to Your Life!

There's no magic to using spices and herbs. Of course, we all have our regular "comfort" flavors that we keep going back to, like salt, pepper, onion, and garlic. If you like those . . . fine. But if you're looking for a change, start by using the spices that came in your spice rack. **There are so many herb and spice choices that can give new excitement to food.** Here are some tips for enjoying them:

- Buy a new herb or spice each time you go shopping. That way you'll get to experiment with ginger one week, sage another, and so on. It'll sure take the ho-hum out of cooking!
- Look through your cookbooks and find recipes that call for herbs or spices that you don't usually use. Then get the new one(s) and go for it! You might find a new family favorite!
- You can substitute dry herbs for fresh with this formula: 1 teaspoon of a dry herb is generally equal to 1 tablespoon of the same chopped fresh herb.
- Don't store dry spices and herbs over your stove or refrigerator. The heat will affect the freshness.

continued

- Dry herbs and spices don't last forever. I bet if you look through your cabinets, you'll find some that go back four or five years. It's hard to believe, but most herbs and spices lose their full strength after one year. So, with that in mind, maybe it's time to start replacing those old ones.

Here are some herbs and complementary combinations to give you a helping hand to get started on your new taste adventures:

FRESH HERB CHART

Herb	Complementary Foods	Complementary Herbs
Basil	Tomatoes, tomato sauces, pasta, salads, fish, eggs, lamb, vegetables	Oregano, parsley, marjoram, thyme, mint, savory, chives
Chives	Carrots, cheese, eggs, fish, potatoes, green salads, soups, spinach, tomatoes	Basil, coriander, dill, marjoram, oregano, parsley, tarragon, thyme
Coriander (Cilantro)	Bread, cheese, chicken, eggs, fish, lamb, mushrooms, pork, green salads, soups, tomatoes	Chives, garlic, marjoram, oregano, parsley
Dill	Veal, chicken, fish, eggs, bread, potatoes, cucumbers, most vegetables, yogurt, sour cream, mustard	Tarragon, rosemary, marjoram, thyme, chives

Kitchen Basics

Herb	Use with	Combines with
Marjoram	Green beans, beef, cauliflower, eggplant, eggs, fish, mushrooms, soups, squash, stuffing, veal, poultry	Basil, bay leaf, chives, coriander, garlic, oregano, mint, parsley, rosemary, sage, savory, thyme
Mint	Carrots, chicken, fruit, frosted beverages, lamb, salads, peas, potatoes	Basil, parsley, tarragon
Oregano	Beef, eggs, fish, lamb, pork, potatoes, salads, stews, tomatoes, veal, vegetables	Basil, bay leaf, chives, coriander, garlic, marjoram, mint, parsley, savory, thyme
Rosemary	Beef, bread, cauliflower, chicken, eggs, lamb, tomatoes, turkey, veal	Savory, thyme, sage
Sage	Dried beans, beef, bread, cheese, eggs, fish, soup, stuffing, turkey	Bay leaf, garlic, marjoram, oregano, parsley, rosemary, savory, thyme
Tarragon	Beef, eggs, fish, lamb, potatoes, salads, tomatoes, turkey, vegetables	Parsley, chives, bay leaf, dill, garlic, mint, savory
Thyme	Dried and green beans, beef, cheese, chicken, eggplant, eggs, fish, lamb	Basil, bay leaf, chives, garlic, marjoram, oregano, parsley, rosemary, sage, savory, tarragon

Compliments of Goodness Gardens

Kitchen Basics

This can make it a little easier to get creative and adventurous (and playful)!

SEASONING COMBINATIONS

Poultry

Rosemary and thyme
Tarragon, marjoram, and onion and garlic powders
Cumin, bay leaf, and saffron or turmeric
Ginger, cinnamon, and allspice
Curry powder, thyme, and onion powder

Beef

Thyme, bay leaf, and instant minced onion
Ginger, dry mustard, and garlic powder
Dill, nutmeg, and allspice
Black pepper, bay leaf, and cloves
Chili powder, cinnamon, and oregano

Pork

Caraway seed, red pepper, and paprika
Thyme, dry mustard, and sage
Oregano and bay leaf
Anise, ginger, and sesame seed
Tarragon, bay leaf, and instant minced garlic

Fish and Seafood

Cumin and oregano
Tarragon, thyme, parsley flakes, and garlic powder
Thyme, fennel, saffron, and red pepper
Ginger, sesame seed, and white pepper
Coriander (cilantro), parsley flakes, cumin, and garlic powder

Kitchen Basics

Potatoes

Dill, onion powder, and parsley flakes
Caraway seed and onion powder
Nutmeg and chives

Rice

Chili powder and cumin
Curry powder, ginger, and coriander (cilantro)
Cinnamon, cardamom, and cloves

Pasta

Basil, rosemary, and parsley flakes
Cumin, turmeric, and red pepper
Oregano and thyme

Vegetables

Green beans: marjoram and rosemary; caraway seed and dry mustard
Broccoli: ginger and garlic powder; sesame seed and nutmeg
Cabbage: celery seed and dill; curry powder and nutmeg
Carrots: cinnamon and nutmeg; ginger and onion powder
Corn: chili powder and cumin; dill and onion powder
Peas: anise and onion powder; rosemary and marjoram
Spinach: curry powder and ginger; nutmeg and garlic powder
Summer squash: mint and parsley flakes, tarragon and garlic powder
Winter squash: cinnamon and nutmeg; allspice and red pepper
Tomatoes: basil and rosemary; cinnamon and ginger

Kitchen Basics

Fruits

Apples: cinnamon, allspice, and nutmeg; ginger and curry powder
Bananas: allspice and cinnamon; nutmeg and ginger
Peaches: coriander (cilantro) and mint; cinnamon and ginger
Oranges: cinnamon and cloves; poppy seed and onion powder
Pears: ginger and cardamom; black or red pepper and cinnamon
Cranberries: allspice and coriander (cilantro); cinnamon and dry mustard
Strawberries or Kiwi fruit: cinnamon and ginger; black pepper and nutmeg

---

NOTE: Black pepper may be used routinely in all dishes, including some fruits, as a basic seasoning. When listed in this chart, it's intended to be a major flavoring.

For best flavor results, keep spices in tightly covered containers, away from heat and light. Check them regularly. As soon as they lose their aroma and color they should be replaced.

Compliments of The American Spice Trade Association

Food Storage Tips

Problem: Over the years I've shared so many quick, easy recipes on my TV show and in my cookbooks. **There have been dishes that were stored in the refrigerator, the freezer, the cookie jar, on the countertop, and the pantry shelf. I think it's about time I shared some tips on the best containers for storing all these goodies!**

What's in Store?

With the thousands of yummy foods that are out there, there are also lots of different ways to store food. Of course, some special creations need special storage attention, but there are some general pointers that should be followed for most foods:

- The most important factor to keep in mind is health. That means temperature. If a food item is supposed to be served cold, then make sure it is kept refrigerated or in a proper thermal container with ice packs—or, for traveling, freeze it and let it thaw on the way to the event. There are also thermal bags, coolers, and other insulated containers for hot and cold foods. Make sure the ones you buy are made for the types of foods you put in them.
- Don't place foods in direct sunlight and don't leave foods sitting out *anywhere* for an extended period of time. Eat it and get leftovers back to the ideal temperature right away. Refrigerated food should be kept at 38°F. to 40°F. and frozen food should be kept at −10°F. to +20°F.

continued

Kitchen Basics

- Some foods, like mushrooms and strawberries, maintain their freshness when stored uncovered, allowing air to circulate around them. Most others are best stored in airtight containers. And when freezing items, be sure they're wrapped in airtight containers so they don't become freezer-burned or pick up unwanted tastes from the freezer. The same goes for most refrigerated items, too—I mean, no one wants cream pie that tastes like onions or blue cheese!
- All food should be stored in containers that work best for the particular items. Choose containers that withstand the temperatures of the items being stored in them. That means that hot soup shouldn't be poured into a thin plastic container (most likely, it will melt). And baked goods shouldn't be frozen on uncoated cardboard because they'll pick up a cardboard taste.
- Glass or ceramic baking dishes work well for most food storage. Many available today can even go from freezer to oven or microwave—but always check the manufacturer's recommendations for intended uses.
- Plastic is a super storage material. Plastic food containers from certain foods, like butter and cottage cheese, can be reused for storing food in the pantry, refrigerator, or freezer, provided they're cleaned thoroughly first and they continue to seal well. Certain deep-colored foods (like tomato sauce) may stain plastic containers, permanently discoloring them. Foods with strong smells, like onions, may leave plastic containers with odors that are difficult to remove. For these foods, choose containers other than plastic.
- Plastic bags, with either a zipper or twist type of closure, are good for storing certain foods because they don't take

Kitchen Basics

up a lot of room and are soft and moldable, which means they can fit into places that larger, hard containers won't.

- Many food items can be refrigerated in cooking pots if the pots are coated with an enamel or nonstick surface or are tempered glass. Many metal pots, like stainless-steel ones, are great for storing food, unless the food has a tomato or other acid base. (The acid in the pots will react with those foods, giving them a metallic taste.) It's best to use glass for those items.
- Be certain to choose the right size container. Leave about 10 percent extra room in a container when freezing, because the food will swell and could burst open an overfull container. Also, choosing a container that's too large will allow frost to form inside the container, which will result in freezer-burned food. (Packing in too-large containers wastes valuable storage space, too.)
- If you are using plastic wrap for freezing food, I recommend wrapping with an outer layer of aluminum foil. This will act as a protective layer to prevent freezer burn. Yes, the special freezer bags and wraps available in most supermarkets work well, too.
- Once you've wrapped your food you've got to remember to label and date it (and include the year). That's the best way to be sure to use leftovers instead of ending up with "mystery" balls of foil in the fridge or freezer that everyone's afraid to open! Sure, you can buy labels, but I usually use good old masking tape and a permanent marker. That way, if the label gets wet, I can still read it!
- Cakes, cookies, and breads that sit out on counters should be kept tightly wrapped. It's okay to keep certain cookies in

continued

Kitchen Basics

a cookie jar, but I recommend a layer of plastic wrap between the top of the jar and the lid to help lock in the freshness. Keep cheesecakes, cream cakes, and other similar cakes and cookies tightly wrapped in the fridge.
- Always keep aluminum foil, waxed paper, storage bags, and sandwich bags on hand. You'll find that they're a valuable part of cooking. After all, fresh *is* best!

Measuring Up:
A Guide to Easy Food Measurement

Problem: Are you one of the many people who likes to have a chart close by for checking measurements? It's sure easier for all of us to have a way to check how many teaspoons are in a tablespoon (3), how many cups are in a quart (4), and so on. I like to include a helpful measuring guide in all of my books, so mark this page because you'll be coming back to it again and again!

QUICK MEASURES

Equals

Dash	Less than 1/8 teaspoon
3 teaspoons	1 tablespoon
4 tablespoons	1/4 cup
5 tablespoons plus 1 teaspoon	1/3 cup
6 tablespoons	3/8 cup
8 tablespoons	1/2 cup
10 tablespoons plus 2 teaspoons	2/3 cup
12 tablespoons	3/4 cup
16 tablespoons	1 cup
2 tablespoons	1 fluid ounce
1 cup	1/2 pint or 8 fluid ounces
2 cups	1 pint or 16 fluid ounces
4 cups	2 pints or 1 quart or 32 fluid ounces
4 quarts	1 gallon or 128 fluid ounces
2 tablespoons fat or butter	1 ounce

continued

Kitchen Basics

¼ pound (1 stick) butter	½ cup
½ pound butter	1 cup
Juice of 1 lemon	About 3 tablespoons
1 cup lemon juice	Juice of 4 to 6 lemons
Juice of 1 orange	About ½ cup
Grated peel of 1 lemon	About 1½ teaspoons
Grated peel of 1 orange	About 1 tablespoon

1 Pound* of	Equals approximately
Flour	4 cups
Cornmeal	3 cups
Cornstarch	3 cups
Granulated sugar	2 cups
Brown sugar	3 cups
Confectioners' sugar	3½ cups
Raisins	3 cups
Rice	2 cups
Macaroni	4 cups
Meat	2 cups, chopped
Diced cooked chicken	3 cups
Potatoes	2 cups, diced, or 3 to 4 medium potatoes
Chopped onions	3 cups
Cheese	4 cups, grated
Bananas	3 medium
Ground coffee	3½ cups

*One pound equals 16 ounces avoirdupois (our usual standard of weight measurement).

How to Get the Most Kitchen Help from Aluminum Foil

Problem: My family used to tease me about one of my kitchen habits . . . and no, it had nothing to do with my cooking! They used to say that **if I ever ran out of aluminum foil, they probably wouldn't get anything to eat until I got back from the store with more!**

Foiled Again!

Okay, my family likes to pick on me. But they're right—I do think aluminum foil is a kitchen necessity. It can go directly from the freezer to the oven. And do you know how much it can cut your cleanup? (I'm a fan of anything that cuts down on cleanup!) Here are a few ways I use this shiny kitchen helper:

- Foil comes in different lengths, as well as in thicknesses from light to extra heavy. Select a foil that's heavy enough for the job. There's no need to use heavy-duty (which costs more) for lighter jobs. Lighter-strength foil is good for freezing or covering small casseroles while cooking. Heavier-strength foil is good for covering large roasts and turkeys, and for grilling. The extra weight helps the foil hold its shape.
- You can use either the shiny or the dull side of aluminum foil against your food—there is no difference in how they work. Using foil to cover roasts, roasting chicken, and casseroles tends to give you moister finished dishes because the

continued

Kitchen Basics

foil traps the steam in and prevents the food from browning too quickly. But make sure to uncover the item for its last 15 minutes of cooking so that it browns. You can also add a few slits to the foil to allow some steam to escape during cooking.

- Line roasting pans and cake pans with lightweight foil. It makes it so much easier to remove sticky cakes and other items from baking pans. And boy, oh boy, does it cut down on cleanup! When your items are done cooking or baking, you just have to lift out the foil and throw away the mess.
- Aluminum foil is a great insulator. Use it to wrap cold soda cans for lunch. It helps keep your whole lunch colder.
- If you need a quick trivet or hot plate, wrap some foil around folded newspaper. The newspaper acts as a pad and the foil protects the paper from moisture and heat (and it can be decorative, too).
- Can't find your funnel? No problem. Roll some foil to create one. It's easy to do and the ends can be made to the exact sizes you need.
- Please, please **be careful when using aluminum foil around electrical outlets or appliances.** Foil is metal and metal conducts electricity. **Do not touch foil to anything electrical.**

Wrapped-Up Cornish Hens

4 servings

Wrapping these Cornish hens in foil makes them juicy. Finishing them on the grill makes them crispy. Doing both makes this a real barbecue treat!

2 Cornish hens (1 pound each)
1 cup orange juice
½ cup honey
2 tablespoons lemon juice
¼ cup (½ stick) butter, melted
1 teaspoon seasoned salt
2 teaspoons ground cinnamon

Wash the Cornish hens with cold water and pat dry with paper towels. Split in half and set aside. Combine the remaining ingredients in a medium-sized bowl and mix well. Dip the hen halves into the mixture, coating evenly. Place 2 halves in a 20"-long piece of heavy-duty aluminum foil and the other 2 halves in another piece of foil. Pour the leftover mixture over the hens and wrap tightly. Place on a preheated barbecue grill over medium-high heat and cook for 30 minutes. Remove the hens from the foil and place on the grill, discarding any remaining liquid. Cook the hens for another 7 minutes per side, or until the skin is crispy and the juices run clear.

Creating Your Own Cookie Cutters

Problem: Holiday time is cookie time. It's a time for fun in the kitchen and creativity on your dessert trays. That's why rolled cookies are so popular at the holidays. But **did you ever get ready to make your holiday goodies and find yourself looking all over for your cookie cutters? Or are you tired of using the same old shapes?** Well, there are lots of things around the kitchen that'll save you.

New Ways to Be on the Cutting Edge

Move over cookie cutters! **Here comes the answer to always having cookie cutters at your fingertips, 'cause these things are always on your kitchen shelves:**

- Clean an empty frozen juice can. Use the open end to cut out perfect circles. Or you can squeeze the end of the can to make oval shapes. They're perfect for egg-shaped cookies at Eastertime!
- Use the open end of drinking glasses for cutting dough. Then try using a smaller glass or a knife to cut a smaller circle inside the first circle for a ring shape. At Christmastime they can be the beginning of wreath cookies.
- Use a sharp knife to cut dough freehand that has been rolled on a cutting board.
- Using a sharp knife, trace clean household objects to make duplicate cutouts (again, only if dough has been rolled on a cutting board)!

Sugar Cookies

5 to 6 dozen

Here's your chance to make some unusual-shaped cookies. Use fun cookie cutters, an ice cream scoop, a frozen juice container, an egg chopper, and even a sharp knife for tracing fun shapes. Have a ball!

1 cup sugar
1 cup (2 sticks) butter, softened
3 tablespoons milk
1 teaspoon vanilla extract

1 egg
3 cups all-purpose flour
1½ teaspoons baking powder
½ teaspoon salt

In a large bowl, combine the sugar, butter, milk, vanilla, and egg until well mixed. Stir in the flour, baking powder, and salt; mix well. Cover with plastic wrap and refrigerate for 1 hour. Preheat the oven to 375°F. On a lightly floured surface, roll out ¼ of the dough at a time to ⅛-inch thickness. Keep the remaining dough refrigerated. Cut out shapes with cookie cutters, different kitchen utensils or gadgets and place on cookie sheets that have been coated with nonstick vegetable spray. Bake for 6 to 9 minutes or until the edges are lightly browned. Repeat until all the dough is used.

Tips for Storing Fresh Onions

Problem: Red, Vidalia, Walla Walla, Maui, Spanish... there are so many varieties of onions to choose from these days! **And with all the choices comes the problem of how to store them.**

Onion Stowaways

- Unless you're planning to use them right away, it's best not to refrigerate fresh onions.
- Onions shouldn't be stored with potatoes because they both give off gases and the gases from one will spoil the other.
- Some of the sweeter, moister types of onions will last longer if they're stored in a way that keeps them from touching each other.
- Onions need ventilation, so storing them in plastic bags is a no-no.
- It's not a good idea to stack onions on top of each other on the floor.

So, what is the best way to store onions? In panty hose! They're the perfect onion storage container! The material allows the onions to breathe. Maybe hang them on a porch or in another well-ventilated area. And to keep them from touching each other, just put the first one into the toe and tie a knot over it. Add another and tie another knot, and so on. (And maybe you could do red onions in one leg and white onions in the other?!) Try it! I think you'll agree it's a "toe-rific" idea!

Onion Strings

3 to 4 servings

We all like onions in soup and along with other foods. But here's a way to enjoy onions by themselves. You'll love 'em!

1 large onion, thinly sliced
1 cup all-purpose flour
1½ teaspoons salt
½ teaspoon white pepper
1 cup vegetable oil

Separate the onion slices into rings. In a medium-sized bowl, combine the flour, salt, and pepper, and mix well. In a large skillet, heat the oil over medium-high heat. Place the onion rings in the flour, coating well, then carefully place them in the hot oil. Fry for 4 to 6 minutes, until golden brown. Drain on paper towels and serve.

NOTE: These are delicious as is, but you can sprinkle them with some salt if you'd like.

How to Bone a Chicken Breast

Problem: One of the most common questions I'm asked is "Why do boneless chicken breasts cost so much more than the rest of the chicken, even bone-in breasts?"

Got a Bone to Pick?

There's a reason—boneless chicken breasts are a high-demand item because **most people don't want to be bothered boning the breasts themselves.** So we pay for the labor of having someone else do it for us. We know boneless breasts cook in no time. Now it's time to **save yourself a good amount of money, too, by boning them yourself.** And it's easy!

Kitchen Basics

Boning a Whole Chicken Breast

1. Place skin-side down on cutting board with widest part nearest you. With point of knife, cut through white cartilage at neck end of keel bone.

2. Pick up breast and bend back, exposing keel bone.

3. Loosen meat from bone by running thumbs around both sides; pull out bone and cartilage.

4. Working with one side of breast, insert tip of knife under long rib bone inside thin membrane and cut or pull meat from rib cage. Turn breast and repeat on other side.

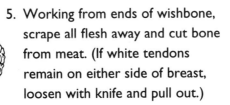

5. Working from ends of wishbone, scrape all flesh away and cut bone from meat. (If white tendons remain on either side of breast, loosen with knife and pull out.)

Courtesy of the National Broiler Council

Kitchen Basics

Boning a Chicken Breast Half

When you buy chicken breasts at the supermarket, they are usually half breasts with four to a package. Remove the bones for fancier and quicker-cooking dishes.

1. Holding breast half in both hands, bend and break keel bone.

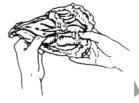

2. Run thumb between meat and keel bone, removing bone and strip of cartilage.

3. Using both thumbs, loosen meat from rib cage.

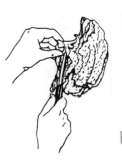

4. Pull or scrape breast meat away from bones. (If small piece of pulley bone remains, pull it out or cut away with knife.)

Courtesy of the National Broiler Council

Russian Chicken

4 to 6 servings

By boning these chicken breasts yourself, you're certainly going to save a bundle. And when you make them like this, they taste restaurant fancy.

3 boneless chicken breasts, each split in half
1 cup sour cream
¾ cup ketchup
¼ cup sweet relish
½ cup sliced celery (about 2 stalks)
1 cup canned French-fried onions

Preheat the oven to 350°F. Rinse the chicken with cold water and pat dry with paper towels; place in a 9" × 13" baking dish that has been coated with nonstick vegetable spray. In a medium-sized bowl, combine the sour cream, ketchup, relish, and celery. Pour the mixture over the chicken and bake, uncovered, for 45 minutes or until the juices run clear, basting occasionally. Remove from the oven and top with the onions before serving.

NOTE: For a real homemade treat, make Onion Strings (page 73) and use those on top instead of the canned onions.

Storage Time for Leftovers

Problem: When holiday time comes, I get lots of questions about **how long leftovers will last in the refrigerator.** These are important questions . . . with even-more-important answers! Read on.

Don't Be Left Out

I've got a chart that can be your guide for holiday (and anytime) leftovers. **In order for this guide to be accurate, foods must be kept covered in a refrigerator at the proper safe temperature zone, which is 38°F. to 40°F. No food should be allowed to sit out at room temperature for more than 2 hours.** This means a total of 2 hours during its lifetime, and doesn't mean 2 hours every time you take it out of the refrigerator. And, of course, **if you have any doubt about whether or not a food is still fresh: BE SAFE AND THROW IT OUT!**

REFRIGERATED LEFTOVER LIFE-TIMES

Cooked turkey	2 days
Cooked ham	3 to 4 days
Cold-cut trays	3 days
Cooked stuffing (outside a bird)	1 to 2 days
Mashed potatoes	1 to 2 days
Cranberry sauce	7 days
Cooked sweet potatoes	7 days
Pumpkin pie	2 to 3 days
Egg nog	4 to 5 days after "sell by" date
Fruitcake	No one knows!

Using Everyday Kitchen Items in All-New Ways

Problem: Your kitchen is stocked with the basics—pots, pans, bowls, and utensils—but sometimes **you'll be making something special and realize you just don't have the right item or the right-sized gizmo when you need it.** Don't worry! Help is here!

Kitchen Double Takes

I've got the answer for those once- or twice-a-year times when you don't really want to go out and buy one more piece of kitchen equipment that you'll hardly ever use. **Use everyday kitchen items in a different way!** Here are a few tips for you to try the next time you get stuck looking for help and adventure in the kitchen:

- Turn your large shallow roasting pans upside down and use the bottoms the same way you would use flat cookie sheets. This is a real help around holiday time when you're baking lots of cookies.
- Use an angel food or Bundt pan for your next ice mold. Why buy a special mold that you'll use just once in a while?
- If you need a funnel, try cutting an empty plastic ketchup bottle in half, keeping the top half and washing it completely. There you go . . . a new funnel.
- Use plastic butter, margarine, and cottage cheese containers as reusable food storage containers for those times when you have more leftovers than containers!

**Kitchen Basics**

- Place your cutting board over your sink, overlapping the counter on each side, when you need to extend your countertop work area.
- Use a rolling pin to help flatten chicken before cooking (it cuts down on cooking time!) or to crush cookies in a plastic bag (for making cookie crumbs—see page 140 for tips on using them).
- Use a fork to prick cuts of meat before cooking. Piercing meat helps break down the muscle and fiber, making it more tender.

Cookie Cups

about 16 cups

Try flipping your muffin tins over and using the bottoms to make edible cookie cups. What colorful, fun treats you can make by filling them with lots of different fillings! The combinations are endless...

1 package (18 to 20 ounces) refrigerated cookie dough, any flavor

Assorted fillings

Freeze the packaged dough for at least an hour, until firm. Preheat the oven to 350°F. Turn a regular-sized muffin tin (or tins) upside down and spray the bottom(s) with nonstick vegetable spray. Slice the firm dough into ½-inch slices and place a slice on each cup. Bake for 11 to 13 minutes, until the dough has baked around the cups and turned golden brown. Cool the cups for 5 to 10 minutes before carefully removing them from the pan(s).

NOTE: The cups are very delicate, so remove them gently. If any do break, it's not a problem—just eat those plain as regular cookies. It's a great way to sample them ahead of time! Fill sugar cookie cups with pie filling or fresh-cut fruit and whipped cream for individual pies. Or how about making chocolate chip cookie cups and filling them with chocolate pudding? WOW!

Easy Tips for Keeping Your Kitchen Clean

Problem: When I stopped to pick up a friend recently I peeked into his kitchen to say hi to his wife and found her in the middle of a disaster zone! There were burned pots on the stove, dirty mixing bowls all around, and it smelled funny! **She was frantic because she was having some friends over in an hour and the place was a mess.** What could she have done to prevent it from getting out of hand?

Don't Get Caught with Your Pans Down

Forget the past—we've all had kitchen disasters. But with a few simple shortcuts, you can say good-bye to long cleanups and hello to fun in the kitchen.

- Always clean up and organize as you prepare and cook. Wash pots and pans when you finish with them, or at least stack them neatly on the counter next to the sink. (If you pile them all in the sink there'll be no room for washing anything.)
- Have cleaning supplies on hand. You can't get grease off your dishes if you don't have any dish detergent! Other musts are a drainboard, sponge, and scouring pad. (To prevent your scouring pad from rusting, store it in a wide-mouthed bottle or glass, and fill with a concentrated soap and water solution, enough to just cover the pad.)
- Use nonstick vegetable spray on pots and pans whenever possible. After cooking, if a pot or pan still has stubborn baked-on food, fill it partway with a soap and water solution

continued

Kitchen Basics

and simmer it on the stove (over low heat) for about 5 minutes. Pour off the water and the burned food should pour out easily, too. For a really burned-on food mess, add a couple of tablespoons of baking soda to the pan with a cup or two of water and simmer until the stain loosens.

- After pots are washed they need to be wiped and put away. Make sure to wipe them well. And for items like metal colanders and muffin tins, try placing them in a warm oven for a few minutes to help them dry completely. (For the bottom of copper pots that you forgot to polish—use either copper cleaner or a paste of salt and vinegar to make the copper bottoms shiny bright in a jiffy.)
- If you're lucky enough to have a dishwasher, put small dirty dishes right into it as you finish with them. Turn it on before the meal so that you can empty it and have room for the dirty dishes after the meal. If you don't have a dishwasher, wash as many dishes as you can while preparing your meal. I don't recommend putting everything in the dishwasher, anyway. Fine china, wooden bowls and spoons, and plasticware may be better off washed by hand. (Washing certain items in the dishwasher may break them, cloud their appearance, and/or warp their shape.) Always check the instructions on items before cleaning them in an automatic dishwasher.
- Place a damp dishtowel under your cutting board before cutting on it. This should stop it from sliding around the counter, and it should also absorb any liquid that goes over the edges of the board. (To remove odors from a cutting board, rub it with the cut side of a lemon.)
- If you haven't cleaned your coffeemaker lately, try this before making your coffee. Add a tablespoon of vinegar to a pot of water and pour it into the coffeemaker. Let it go

Kitchen Basics

through the brew cycle, then pour out the mixture. Put a pot of clear tap water through a brew cycle, then pour that out. That should help clean out the system.

- Okay, you've got the kitchen looking pretty good, but it has a funny smell. Put a cup of water in a saucepan with a few cloves and either ground cinnamon or a cinnamon stick and let it simmer for 5 to 10 minutes. It'll freshen the air naturally. (And the next time you cook cauliflower or some other strong-smelling vegetable, add a slice of bread to the cooking water to absorb the odor.)

Your guests will arrive and be amazed that you were able to prepare a delicious meal *and* have a neat, fresh-smelling kitchen besides! Congratulations!

Time and Money Savers

Isn't it amazing? Every time I talk about saving time or money, everybody pays attention! Well, sure they do—because today none of us can afford to waste either one!

I hate to waste any parts of food, so it's almost a game for me to figure out what to do with parts that we don't usually use—like the fruit juice left in the canned pineapple or peaches (or other fruit) after we eat the fruit (page 164) . . . and the peanut butter and honey that just don't want to come out of the measuring cup after we measure them for a recipe (page 107).

I also hate to spend money for food, only to find that I can't eat it—like meat that's too tough. That's why I included Tricks for Meat Lovers (page 114). And when it comes to using up that bumper crop of tomatoes from our gardens . . . ? I've got a way to do that, too (page 96)!

Since most of us are short on cooking time, but still want to make homemade meals, I've got some suggestions for doing that—but in less time! See my tips on cooking in double batches (page 90), using canned beans to make Quick Black Bean Soup (page 102), making one-dish meals (page 111), and more!

So, get going! There's no time or money to waste!

Contents

Time and Money Savers

Cooking in Double Batches	90
Recipe: Double Delicious Chili	92
Bread Crumb Alternatives	93
Recipe: Crispy Chicken	95
Finally, a Way to Use That Bumper Crop of Tomatoes!	96
Recipe: Blender Tomato Sauce	98
Minced Garlic in No Time	99
Recipe: Italian Garlic Pizza	100
Canned Beans Are Quicker Than Dried	101
Recipe: Quick Black Bean Soup	102
Easy Ways with Refrigerated and Frozen Bread Dough	103
Recipes: State Fair Fried Dough	105
Mexican Biscuit Bake	106

Time and Money Savers

Stop Ingredients from Sticking to Measuring Cups	107
Recipe: Peanut Butter Cup Surprises	108
Shortening Pasta Preparation Time	109
Recipe: Macaroni and Cheese Pie	110
One-Dish Meals Mean Less Work	111
Recipe: Tomorrow's Shepherd's Pie	112
How to Cook Less-Expensive Meat Cuts	114
Recipe: Cola Roast	116
Go Ahead... Buy Convenience Foods!	117
Recipe: Vegetable Fried Rice	119
Canned Meats, Chicken, and Fish Save the Day	120
Recipe: Open-Faced Chicken Oscar	122
How to Cut Cooking and Baking Times	123
Recipe: Muffin Tin Meat Loaves	125
Make Soup in No Time	126
Recipe: Quick Vegetable Soup	128
Make Your Kitchen a Pizzeria	129
Recipe: Quick and Easy Pizza	131

Time and Money Savers

How to Get the Most from Fresh Strawberries	132
Recipe: Summer Strawberry Sauce	134
Tips for Sprucing Up Packaged Food Mixes	135
Recipe: Pineapple Upside-Down Cake	137
Quick Deglazing	138
Recipe: French-Glazed Chicken	139
What to Do with Cookie Crumbs	140
Recipe: Cookie Pie Crust	141

Cooking in Double Batches

Problem: Wouldn't it be nice to come home from work or school and have dinner ready? All you'd have to do is pop it in the oven! You could have a night free from long lists of ingredients and all cooking. Could this be a dream?!

Cook Once, Eat Twice (or More!)

You can make your dream come true with a really simple idea: cooking in double batches! When you're already cooking, what's the big deal about making twice as much?! Sure, when you're buying whatever you need for your favorite dishes, just buy for making it twice. Then, after you cook both batches, just freeze half for dinner sometime later in the month. The best part is, if you plan right, you can have homemade meals ready-to-go in the freezer. Now, this tip won't work for every recipe, but I usually suggest it for our heartier meals. The following dishes are just as flavorful the second time around, meaning that you can be a winner twice by cooking only once:

- Lasagna and other saucy Italian dishes
- Macaroni and cheese or casseroles with cheese
- Stews and pot roasts
- Fried and roasted chicken—simply thaw and reheat in a hot oven and you'll be enjoying crispy chicken again in no time.
- Meat loaf—a batch from the freezer with some fresh gravy . . . yummy!

Time and Money Savers

- Even prepared raw chicken breasts—you know, skinned and boned (and even breaded)—can be real time-savers. All you have to do is wrap and freeze them for when you need a quick dinner. Then just unwrap them and pop them in a 350°F. oven right from the freezer.
- Soups—who says soup can't be an awesome dinner?

Double Delicious Chili

12 servings (or enough for 6 servings two times!)

Why not make this double batch of chili? Then you'll have one for now and one for later—you know, when you'll want something homemade but won't want to cook!

- 2 pounds ground beef
- 1 large onion, chopped (2½ cups)
- 1 can (28 ounces) crushed tomatoes
- 1 can (28 ounces) whole tomatoes, quartered
- 2 cans (15½ ounces each) red kidney beans, drained
- 2 tablespoons chili powder
- 1 teaspoon salt
- 1 teaspoon pepper

In a large skillet, sauté the ground beef over medium-high heat until lightly browned; add the onion and continue cooking until the beef is completely browned and the onion is golden. Drain the liquid and place the mixture in a large saucepan. Reduce the heat to low, add the remaining ingredients, and simmer for 50 to 60 minutes, stirring occasionally.

NOTE: I know that traditional chili recipes don't include kidney beans, but lots of people like them in their chili, and they make it so much heartier!

Bread Crumb Alternatives

Problem: The last time my wife went to make us some fried chicken, she spent lots of time looking in the cupboards for bread crumbs. But she finally closed them and announced that we'd be having something else for dinner that night. Fried chicken is one of my favorites, so I was disappointed. But **when I asked her why we couldn't have it, and she told me we were out of bread crumbs, I told her we were still in luck!** Know why?

No Bread Crumbs? No Problem!

There are lots of things we can use in place of bread crumbs! Sometimes we get so used to making things the same way every time that we think we can't make them if we don't have exactly what the recipe calls for. Well, with bread crumbs there are lots of easy options! I've tried all of these, and they all work just as well. Do your own experiments:

- Crushed potato chips in any flavor or style, from regular to spicy, and plain to ridged (a crunchy addition to the breading lineup)
- Cracker crumbs or crushed crackers (a super flavor addition to whatever food you're breading!)
- Crushed breakfast cereals in rice, wheat, oat, unsweetened, or sweetened varieties (a nice flavor booster)
- Crushed snack foods like pretzels and corn chips (you'll be surprised by how much they perk up the flavor of breaded foods)

continued

To make crumbs from any of those:
- Place a cup or so of the item into a food processor with a cutting blade and process for about 30 seconds, or until it reaches the desired consistency.

OR:

- Place the item in a plastic bag, seal tightly, and roll it with a rolling pin until crushed completely.

Give these crumbs a try—even when you're *not* out of bread crumbs. You'll have a whole new way to coat and flavor your foods.

Crispy Chicken

6 to 8 servings

You can use other cereal or snack food crumbs with this one—and by changing the crumbs each time you make it, you can give it a new "coat" every time!

- 3 cups crispy rice cereal, crushed
- 1 tablespoon dried parsley flakes
- 1 teaspoon onion powder
- ½ teaspoon garlic powder
- ½ teaspoon dried oregano
- ½ teaspoon salt
- ¼ teaspoon pepper
- 2 eggs
- 1 tablespoon water
- 4 boneless and skinless chicken breasts (1¼ to 1½ pounds), pounded to about ⅓" thick
- 2 tablespoons vegetable oil

Preheat the oven to 350°F. In a medium-sized bowl, combine the cereal crumbs, parsley flakes, onion powder, garlic powder, oregano, salt, and pepper until well mixed. In a shallow bowl, beat the eggs and water with a fork. Dip the chicken into the egg mixture, then into the crumb mixture, coating completely. Spread the oil on a large rimmed cookie sheet and bake the chicken for 30 to 35 minutes, or until lightly browned and the juices run clear.

Finally, a Way to Use That Bumper Crop of Tomatoes!

Problem: I have friends who live in an apartment and decided to try growing several tomato plants on their patio. Well, the results were overwhelming! **They had more tomatoes than they knew what to do with, even after they gave a bunch to their neighbors and friends. Their kitchen counter was constantly overflowing with tomatoes that would soften before they could be eaten.** What did I tell them to do?

You Say "Tomato" ...I Say "Tomato Sauce"

With the right growing conditions anyone can end up with a bumper tomato crop. If you harvest more than you can handle, here are a few tips on how to enjoy them all:

- Try cutting the tomatoes in half and sprinkling them with herbs and shredded cheese, then broiling them for 3 to 4 minutes. What a great side dish!
- Cut up firm tomatoes and toss with chunks of onions and bottled Italian dressing for a quick, refreshing tomato salad.
- Try adding fresh tomato chunks to your favorite casseroles and stews. And fresh tomato slices make a hearty extra layer in lasagna. WOW! What an exciting boost for almost any dish!

Time and Money Savers

- Don't forget sandwiches! With a bumper crop, it would be a sin not to top off any sandwich with a thick slice of garden-fresh tomato.
- If you want to peel tomatoes for freezing or canning, dip them into a pot of boiling water for 1 to 2 minutes, then remove them with a slotted spoon. Cool slightly; then the skins should zip right off!

Blender Tomato Sauce

about 4½ cups

Why not turn your extra fresh tomatoes into tomato sauce in no time? You won't want any other sauce once you taste the garden freshness of this one!

4 pounds very ripe tomatoes, chunked
½ teaspoon dried oregano
½ teaspoon dried basil
½ teaspoon garlic powder
1 teaspoon sugar
1 teaspoon salt
¼ teaspoon black pepper

Place half of the tomato chunks in a blender and blend until a smooth liquid. Pour the liquid into a medium-sized saucepan. Blend the other half of the tomatoes and pour into the saucepan. Add the remaining ingredients and cover. Simmer for about 1 hour, stirring occasionally.

NOTE: When cool, place the sauce in plastic containers and freeze in usable amounts for up to 6 months.

Minced Garlic in No Time

Problem: You want to make a recipe that calls for finely chopped or minced fresh garlic, but **it always seems like so much work and waste to chop it the traditional way** with a knife and cutting board. It seems like you end up with more garlic on the knife, board, and your hands than you do in the recipe! And what a lot of cleanup for such a little amount of garlic!

Chopping with a Fork?!

I found a quick trick for finely chopping and mincing a small amount of garlic, and you don't even need a knife or a cutting board. Simply separate and peel a clove of garlic from the bulb and hold the end of it with your fingers. Next, on a plate or in a shallow bowl, **rub the garlic with the tines of a fork, sort of mashing it.** That's it! Well, now that you can have chopped garlic with no work, I'm sure you'll be having it more often. So here are some suggestions for ways to enjoy it:

- Add fresh mashed garlic to butter and spread it on Italian or French bread. Broil it until golden brown and you'll have great garlic bread in no time.
- Add fresh mashed garlic to your favorite jarred spaghetti sauce for an extra "Wow"! Your family will think it's your own new signature sauce.
- Add a teaspoon or two of fresh mashed garlic to your favorite homemade or bottled Italian dressing, give it a shake, and it's ready to serve. (Make sure you have some breath mints on hand!)

Italian Garlic Pizza

6 to 8 servings

Everyone seems to love garlic pizza, so make sure you give them the garlic zing they're looking for when you make this Italian specialty!

5 cloves garlic, mashed
¼ cup (½ stick) butter, melted
1 12" to 14" fresh, packaged, or frozen (thawed) prepared pizza shell
1 cup (4 ounces) shredded mozzarella cheese
1 teaspoon chopped fresh parsley

Preheat the oven to 400°F. In a small bowl, combine the garlic and butter. Brush evenly over the prepared pizza shell, then sprinkle evenly with the cheese and parsley. Bake for 15 to 20 minutes, until the cheese is melted and the crust begins to crispen.

NOTE: If you'd like, add some sliced mushrooms, or some chopped onions or bell peppers... maybe even some thinly sliced pepperoni.

Canned Beans Are Quicker Than Dried

Problem: I had friends over a few weeks ago and before dinner I served them a rich bean soup with some crusty bread. Boy, oh boy, did I ever get compliments! And I heard lots of "It must have taken you all day to make a thick bean soup like this!" I just smiled 'cause no one knew how easy it was. **They all said they wished they could make soup like this, but complained, "Who has the time?"**

Time to Spill the Beans

We all do! I'll share my secret 'cause it's not fair for me to be the only kitchen hero with this one. **Use canned beans!** They're already cooked and ready to go. Here are a couple of other quick recipe ideas for canned beans:

- Add canned beans to your pot roast to give it an ethnic flair.
- Purée canned black beans in the food processor with a bit of beef broth to make a hearty sauce for serving over chicken and beef.
- Add drained canned beans to your favorite pasta dish for a real Italian taste.
- Toss 3 or more varieties of drained canned beans together with some fresh chopped veggies (like bell peppers, onions, tomatoes, and celery) and your favorite vinaigrette or Italian dressing for a chilled side salad that's gangbusters!
- Add some puréed canned kidney beans along with whole ones when you want to add body to bean-style chili.

Quick Black Bean Soup

5 servings

The shortcut is in the canned beans, the taste is in the bowls, and the smiles are all around the table!

2 cans (15 ounces each) black beans, drained
1 can (10½ ounces) condensed chicken broth
½ cup water
1 small onion, quartered
2 garlic cloves, minced
1½ teaspoons ground cumin
½ teaspoon dried oregano
2 tablespoons chopped green bell pepper (optional)
4 teaspoons sour cream (optional)

Place the beans, chicken broth, water, onion, garlic, cumin, and oregano in a blender jar or a food processor bowl. Process the ingredients for 1 minute, turn off the processor and wait until the blades stop, then scrape down the sides of the container; process the mixture for another minute, until smooth. Transfer the mixture to a medium-sized saucepan and bring to a boil. Reduce the heat and simmer, uncovered, for 15 minutes, stirring frequently. Place in serving bowls and garnish with chopped bell pepper and sour cream, if desired.

Easy Ways with Refrigerated and Frozen Bread Dough

Problem: There's no smell like the smell of fresh-baked bread. That's a smell that takes me back to when I was a kid and my mom always took me to the local bakery for fresh bread. Well, it's always bothered me that there was **no way to get that smell at home without a** *lot* **of work.** Most of us just **don't have the time or the patience to make bread from scratch today.**

Rolling in the Dough

No problem! **With the variety of refrigerated and frozen bread doughs that are available today we can make all sorts of fresh-tasting treats** . . . and what do you know?! You can get that smell of fresh-baked bread without all the old-time work! Try using the dough as directed on the packages, or experiment in any of these ways:

- For some fun with leftovers, wrap leftover cooked meat or chicken chunks in refrigerator dough and bake until browned. Make them large for your dinner main course or small for snacks or quick hors d'oeuvres.
- Unroll refrigerator dough flat onto a cookie sheet and top with sautéed vegetables and cheese. Bake it and you've got easy homemade pizza. Use crescent rolls for French pizza

continued

Time and Money Savers

and buttermilk biscuit dough for a rich American pizza taste.
- Fold mix-ins like raisins, cinnamon and sugar, herbs, nuts, or seeds (caraway, sesame, or poppy) into thawed frozen bread dough and bake according to the package instructions. (You can tell everybody it's your own special recipe!)

State Fair Fried Dough

30 to 35 pieces

2 cups vegetable oil
1 loaf (1 pound) frozen bread dough, thawed

½ cup granulated sugar

In a large skillet, heat the oil over medium-high heat. Meanwhile, separate the loaf of dough by pulling it apart into 1-inch pieces. Test the oil for readiness by carefully placing 1 piece of dough into the pan. You'll know the oil is ready when the dough bubbles around the edges. Place the remaining pieces of dough into the oil and fry a few at a time until golden brown on the bottom. Then turn the dough over and brown on the other side. Remove from the skillet with a slotted spoon and drain on paper towels. Repeat until all the dough is fried. Place the sugar in a shallow dish or a resealable plastic bag. Roll or shake the fried dough in the sugar to coat completely. Serve hot.

NOTE: BE CAREFUL! The oil will be very hot!

Mexican Biscuit Bake

21 side dish servings

- 2 tablespoons butter or margarine
- 1 large can (17.3 ounces) refrigerated buttermilk biscuits
- 1 small can (10.8 ounces) refrigerated buttermilk biscuits
- 1 jar (16 ounces) medium "thick and chunky" salsa (1¾ cups), plus 1 cup salsa for garnish (optional)
- 3 cups (12 ounces) shredded Monterey Jack cheese
- ½ cup chopped green bell peppers
- ½ cup sliced scallions
- 1 can (2¼ ounces) sliced black olives, drained

Preheat the oven to 375°F. Melt the butter in a 9" × 13" glass baking dish, then evenly coat the baking dish with the butter. Separate all of the biscuit dough into a total of 13 biscuits. Cut each biscuit into eight pieces and place the pieces in a large bowl; toss with the 1¾ cups salsa. Spoon evenly into the butter-coated baking dish. Sprinkle with the cheese, peppers, scallions, and olives. Bake for 35 to 45 minutes, or until the edges are deep golden brown and the center is set. Let stand for 15 minutes, then cut into squares. Serve with additional salsa, if desired.

NOTE: This is a great dinner side dish that's also perfect for lunch or a snack! And don't be afraid to substitute a milder or hotter salsa, or even to use mozzarella cheese instead of Monterey Jack. It'll be like your own Mexican fiesta!

Stop Ingredients from Sticking to Measuring Cups

Problem: I hate waste and I hate lots of cleanup. So one thing that always bothered me was when **recipes called for measuring honey, peanut butter, corn syrup, or other sticky items. Out came my measuring cup, in went my ingredient, and that was where it wanted to stay!** Even after I worked at spooning it out, I think I left a lot in the cup. I knew there had to be a solution!

Measure Your Food, Not How Much You Waste

All you have to do is **spray some nonstick vegetable spray into your measuring cup (or measuring spoons) before putting in any gooey ingredients.** It'll make the item slide out much more easily . . . a sure time-saver and money-saver too, since there's no waste! And you'll be sure to get the right amount into your recipe.

If you don't have any nonstick vegetable spray, then measure your oil or shortening first (if your recipe calls for it)—before your sticky items. That'll make them slide out just as easily.

Peanut Butter Cup Surprises

24 cupcakes

Here's a recipe where you have to measure out peanut butter. Everybody knows how gooey peanut butter is, but with our new trick... WOW! Easy measuring every time!

1¾ cups all-purpose flour
1¼ cups firmly packed brown sugar
3 teaspoons baking powder
1 teaspoon salt
1 cup milk
⅓ cup vegetable shortening
⅓ cup peanut butter
1 teaspoon vanilla extract
2 eggs
24 miniature milk-chocolate–covered peanut butter cups, unwrapped

Preheat the oven to 350°F. Line 24 medium-sized muffin tins with paper baking cups. In a large bowl, combine all the ingredients except the peanut butter cups. With an electric beater, blend at low speed until moistened. Then beat at medium speed for 2 more minutes. Fill the paper-lined muffin cups ⅔ full. Press 1 peanut butter cup into the batter in each muffin cup until the top edge of each candy is even with the top of the batter. Bake for 18 to 20 minutes or until the tops spring back when touched lightly in the center.

NOTE: Serve warm or cool, plain or "fancied up" with sprinkles or frosting!

Shortening Pasta Preparation Time

Problem: I love the old-fashioned tastes of casseroles and other baked pasta dishes—always hot and delicious. **It sure would be easier to make them if we could cut down on some of the steps by not having to cook the pasta first.** Well, I just discovered that I can make them 1-2-3, and with very little mess! Here's how:

Don't Boil That Pasta!

No boiling, rinsing, or draining the pasta first. Simply use raw pasta in the recipe. It's an all-in-one easy that really works. I've got a sure winner here, but go ahead and try it in your favorite casserole or other baked pasta recipe. Just add about double the original amount of liquid to the recipe and bake it, covered, until the liquid is absorbed. Go on and experiment. It'll sure get mealtime here easier and sooner!

Select supermarkets around the country also carry "no-cook" pasta brands. If using those, just follow the package directions for more ways to quicker pasta dishes.

Macaroni and Cheese Pie

6 to 8 servings

Here's a recipe that really works well without precooked pasta. No one will ever know you skipped that step... and you'll wonder why you've wasted all that time up till now!

2 cups (8 ounces) shredded Cheddar cheese, divided
1 cup *uncooked* elbow macaroni
4 eggs
⅛ teaspoon dry mustard
2¼ cups milk
½ cup biscuit baking mix
¼ teaspoon salt
¼ teaspoon pepper

Preheat the oven to 400°F. Grease a 10-inch pie plate. In a medium-sized bowl, combine 1¾ cups cheese and the macaroni; sprinkle into the pie plate. Place the remaining ingredients, except the remaining ¼ cup cheese, in a blender jar and beat until smooth for about 15 seconds on high speed (or for 1 minute in a large bowl with a hand beater). Pour into the pie plate. Bake for about 40 minutes, or until a knife inserted in the center comes out clean. Sprinkle with the remaining ¼ cup cheese. Bake for another 1 to 2 minutes, until the cheese is melted. Cool for 10 minutes, then cut into wedges.

One-Dish Meals Mean Less Work

Problem: We've all been there—we walk in the door after a long, hard day, and before we can even get our coats off, the phone is ringing, the dog is barking, and the kids are starving. **The last thing we feel like doing is lots of chopping, mixing, and cooking! We wish we could just throw something into the oven and have that be it.** No sweat!

We're All for One (Dish, That Is)

My solution for nights like this is **planning.** We know we're not going to have much preparation time tomorrow night, so all we have to do is **have an all-in-one dish prepared in advance.** Then we simply pop it into the oven or microwave when we get home. And we'll have time to be with our families (and solve any of the usual household problems). I'm not saying that we shouldn't plan on cooking quick things some nights, but if we know we're going to have some hectic nights ahead, then it really makes sense to make some goulash, lasagna, or shepherd's pie the weekend or night before. Then we can just make our magic on those busy nights and still know we're bringing a healthy meal to our tables. It's one more way to be a kitchen hero.

Tomorrow's Shepherd's Pie

6 to 8 servings

Shepherd's pie is a baked combination of chopped meat, vegetables, sauce, and mashed potatoes. And if you'd rather have tomato sauce than gravy, try that instead. The pie should be your own creation!

- 1 pound lean ground beef
- 1 cup chopped onion (about 1 large onion)
- 1 envelope (1.15 ounces) onion soup mix
- 1 can (10½ ounces) beef gravy
- 1 teaspoon garlic powder
- ½ teaspoon black pepper
- 1 can (7 ounces) whole kernel corn, drained
- 1 can (16 ounces) sliced carrots, drained
- 1 package (10 ounces) frozen peas, thawed
- 5 cups (8 servings) instant mashed potatoes, prepared according to package directions
- Paprika for sprinkling

Preheat the oven to 350°F. In a large skillet, brown the ground beef and chopped onion. Drain the liquid, if necessary. Add the soup mix, gravy, garlic powder, and pepper; mix well. Add the corn, carrots, and peas. Place in a 2-quart casserole dish that has been coated with nonstick vegetable spray. Spread the mashed potatoes over the top and sprinkle with paprika. Bake for 25 minutes or until heated through. Allow to cool, then cover and store in the refrigerator until just before serving. Then uncover and reheat at 350°F. for 25 to 30 minutes or in the microwave on high power until heated through.

Time and Money Savers

If planning more than 3 days ahead, wrap the pie well and freeze until the night before planning to serve. Let it thaw in the refrigerator overnight, then reheat as above.

NOTE: If you'd like, you can sprinkle ½ cup of your favorite cheese over the potatoes before sprinkling with paprika. And for even quicker preparation, you could use 2 16-ounce bags of frozen mixed vegetables instead of the corn, carrots, and peas.

How to Cook Less-Expensive Meat Cuts

Problem: My family loves meat—thick-cut, thin-cut, steaks, roasts—just about any way it comes. But if it's not prepared and cooked right, it can be way too tough! So, **how do you end up with a tender piece of meat without having to spend a fortune at the meat counter?**

Tricks for Meat Lovers

You don't have to spend a lot of money to enjoy tender cuts of meat. Sure, there's a reason why tenderloin is more expensive than shoulder roast—but if you know a few tricks you can make that less-expensive shoulder roast seem just as tender and tasty as the tenderloin!

- One of the most popular ways to tenderize is by cooking with "moist heat." You know, like we do when we boil our corned beef and cabbage, braise our leg of lamb, or make pot roast on top of the stove or covered in the oven. They all need to be cooked in liquid. And the liquid can be water, chicken or beef broth, and even cola or beer. Cooking meats till they're tender usually means cooking them at lower temperatures for a longer period of time—maybe even 2 or 3 hours—so they end up being fork-tender.
- Raw meats can be tenderized by breaking down the tough fibers. An example of this is cube steak, where needles are run over the meat to change its texture. It can then be pan-fried or braised and is the type of meat used in that popular

Time and Money Savers

dish, Swiss Steak. You can do this technique at home by pounding the meat with a meat mallet on a cutting board on a solid counter. There are also hand-held and other mechanical tenderizers on the market that do a super job. Check your local kitchen supply store.
- Meat can also be tenderized with spice-type or liquid tenderizers that get sprinkled or poured on. They can usually be found in supermarket spice sections.
- When making beef stew (not a roast), try replacing ¼ of your cooking liquid with strong tea. It'll cut down on the cooking time while making the meat more tender.

Cola Roast

8 to 10 servings

A pot of tender meat means a dinner that's not too tough to chew. See how your beef lovers like this one!

- 1 teaspoon salt
- ½ teaspoon pepper
- ½ teaspoon garlic powder
- 1 4- to 5-pound bottom round roast
- 3 tablespoons vegetable oil
- 1 can (12 ounces) cola-flavored soda
- 12 ounces chili sauce
- 2 tablespoons Worcestershire sauce
- 2 tablespoons hot pepper sauce

Preheat the oven to 325°F. In a small bowl, combine the salt, pepper, and garlic powder; rub over the surface of the roast. In a Dutch oven or a soup pot, heat the oil to hot and brown the roast on all sides. Transfer the roast to a roasting pan. In a small bowl, combine the remaining ingredients and pour over the roast. Cover and roast for 2½ to 3 hours or until tender.

Go Ahead... Buy Convenience Foods!

Problem: Since many of us are more health-conscious than ever before, the grocery stores are doing a lot to give us what we want. There seem to be many more choices for us in both whole and cut fresh fruits and vegetables. **Sure, we'd all like to be able to have a never-ending wide assortment of cut fruits and vegetables in our fridge, but it's costly and wasteful.** For instance, if a recipe calls for a bit of broccoli, usually the balance of the bunch isn't enough for a whole meal, so it ends up sitting in the vegetable bin and spoiling before you can figure out what to do with it. How can you avoid so much waste?

Why Not Put a Little "Easy" in Your Life?

Give in and shop for convenience. Why not? Sometimes the cost really isn't any more for convenience items, considering that the waste is minimal. I suggest finding a deli or grocery store that has a salad bar. It's ideal to buy "select" items, and if you do your homework before you go shopping, you can let the store do all the work. Imagine how easy it is to buy vegetables and fruits already cleaned, cut up, and ready for cooking. Now that's what I call teamwork!

continued

Time and Money Savers

Here are a few easy ways with precut veggies and fruit:
- Add precut vegetables to canned soup for a homemade touch.
- Toss cut carrots, celery, and mushrooms with cooked pasta for a fancy Italian specialty. Just add a bit of your favorite dressing, give it a toss, and you're ready to go.
- Toss cut fruit with a splash of orange juice and a bit of lemon-lime soda for a refreshing dessert.

Vegetable Fried Rice

4 servings

Using precut vegetables from a package or a salad bar certainly cuts down on preparation time and waste... and it's easy, too!

3 tablespoons vegetable oil
½ pound (8 ounces) of thin, angle-cut slices of any one or combination of these: broccoli florets, celery, scallions, mushrooms, carrots, red bell peppers

3 cups cold cooked rice
1 tablespoon soy sauce
¼ cup chicken broth
⅛ teaspoon black pepper

In a medium-sized skillet, heat the oil over medium-high heat; add the vegetables and sauté for 5 to 7 minutes. Stir in the rice and sauté for another 5 minutes. Add the soy sauce and stir-fry until the rice is well coated (evenly brown). Add the broth and pepper, remove from the heat, and serve.

NOTE: For fried rice with a "zip," add some hot mustard or a dash of hot pepper sauce. Then it's almost like Szechuan-style fried rice.

Canned Meats, Chicken, and Fish Save the Day

Problem: You know those days when **you open your fridge to see what you can make for dinner and all you have are the side dish staples and nothing for the main course? And there's no time to thaw something? And dinnertime is just minutes away?** Oops! Well, if you've done your homework, you should have no worries.

TIP: "Uncanny" Dinner in a Snap

Why shouldn't you worry? Because you've got canned meat, chicken, or fish in the cupboard. **That's right! Today, with all the hustle and bustle in our lives, we sometimes forget to buy or defrost our main dish item. But we care about putting a good dinner on the table . . . and that's still possible. The assortments of canned meat, chicken, and fish that are available today are really super!**

- Instead of ground beef in meat loaf, use the same amount of canned tuna fish or salmon. You'll have a dynamite new fish loaf for your seafood lovers.
- Canned chunk-style chicken is great tossed with teriyaki sauce and stir-fried vegetables.
- Add canned chunk-style meats to stews, chilis, or casseroles.
- Alternate layers of canned chunk-style ham and chicken with Swiss cheese to make your own version of the French classic Chicken Cordon Bleu.

- You can make substitutions in your creamed dishes, like canned tuna fish in your Seafood Newburg or canned chunk-style chicken in Chicken à la King.
- Canned chunk-style ham is the perfect addition for a quick version of scalloped potatoes and ham, like Mom used to make.

Open-Faced Chicken Oscar

2 to 4 servings

For a quick, easy dish that'll have an "uncanny" appeal for the whole gang, try this one!

¼ cup mayonnaise
⅛ teaspoon black pepper
1 can (10 ounces) chunk-style chicken, drained and flaked
4 slices white or wheat bread, toasted
1⅓ cups frozen asparagus cuts (from a 10-ounce package), thawed and drained
4 slices sandwich-sized Swiss cheese

Preheat the oven to 400°F. In a small bowl, combine the mayonnaise and pepper, then add the flaked chicken. Place the 4 slices of toast on a cookie sheet. Top each slice of toasted bread with ½ cup of the chicken mixture, then top with ⅓ cup of asparagus cuts, and cover with a slice of cheese. Bake for 5 to 8 minutes or until the sandwiches are heated through and the cheese is melted.

NOTE: You don't have to use Swiss cheese if you prefer another kind. Use your favorite.

How to Cut Cooking and Baking Times

Problem: There are more families than ever where both parents work and the kids have tons of after-school activities. That means you're getting home later—closer to dinnertime. **Making home-cooked meals has become a real struggle in recent years. We've got very little preparation time, but we still want to give our families the best dinners possible.** Help has arrived! No more sacrificing quality just because we have so little time!

Tricks for Quicker Meals and Treats

There's a lot we can do to feed our families the way we want to. Try my suggestions so you can say good-bye to long-cooking roasting and baking, and hello to dinner on the table at a reasonable hour. C'mon, you've got everything to gain!

- Cut down on the cooking time for casseroles by making smaller ones and using shallower baking dishes.
- Before cooking, cut roasts into steaks so that dinner is served at dinnertime and not during homework hour and TV prime time!
- Pound chicken breasts thin to reduce the frying, grilling, or roasting time.
- Use cut-up, ready-to-cook chicken parts instead of whole chickens. Pieces cook much faster.

continued

Time and Money Savers

- Make lasagna or baked ziti in advance, in individual-sized portions. Then you just have to reheat and eat!
- When making gelatin, pour it into single-serve glasses or bowls. They'll chill and firm up in less than half the time of one big bowl.
- Instead of baking a cake in a cake pan, pour the batter into muffin cups. You'll end up with quick take-along treats that bake in half the time of cake!

Muffin Tin Meat Loaves

12 meat loaf muffins

By making meat loaf in muffin tins, you reduce the cooking time... which means that dinner can be on the table in a flash. Now, isn't that great news?!

1½ pounds lean ground beef
1½ cups shredded zucchini (about 1 medium-sized zucchini)
1 cup bread crumbs
1 egg, slightly beaten
1 teaspoon dried Italian seasoning
½ teaspoon salt
¼ cup ketchup

Preheat the oven to 400°F. In a large bowl, combine all the ingredients except the ketchup, mixing lightly but thoroughly. Place about ⅓ cup of the beef mixture into each of 12 ungreased medium-sized muffin cups, pressing lightly; spread ketchup over the tops. Bake for 20 minutes or until no pink remains and the juices run clear.

NOTE: Not only is this a quick dinner, but it's a great way for kids of all ages to enjoy all-in-one meat and veggie muffins!

Make Soup in No Time

Problem: It seemed like Grandma always had a pot of soup simmering on the stove. And why not? It didn't come ready-made then like it does today. So she took the time to cut up the chicken, clean and cut the vegetables, and add fresh herbs. She let it cook all day 'cause she was home anyway. **Who has the time to make fresh soup these days? You do!**

Yes, You Can!

Homemade soups are popular again, since people are looking for "homemade hearty" foods. There's also a big trend toward "all-in-one" foods. Well, soup is it! On page 101 I talk about making soup with canned beans, but now I want to go even further and share some hints for making your own version of homemade soup that'll warm your whole gang's tummies without taking up your whole day. Remember, these are just suggestions:

- Start with a stock. It can be chicken, beef, vegetable, or seafood and should be something easy like a canned broth, consommé, or a mixture of hot water and bouillon cubes.
- Add a selection of canned or frozen vegetables. Fresh vegetables are great, too, but it'll take a few more minutes of simmering to make them tender.
- Next, of course, come the seasonings. Use your own selection of fresh or dried herbs or spices from the countless varieties that are available from around the world. (For some recommendations, see the charts on pages 56 to 60.)

Time and Money Savers

You may want to thicken your soup, and there are a number of ways to do that:

- Add raw or cooked rice or pasta to the broth (but not too much because it will expand as it absorbs the liquid). A little goes a long way, so if it thickens the soup too much, then don't be afraid to add some extra water or broth to bring it to the desired consistency.
- Soups can also be thickened with a bit of cornstarch dissolved in cold water and stirred into the hot soup.
- Add some leftover mashed potatoes or gradually stir in some instant potato flakes. Stir until the soup reaches the desired consistency.

Whatever ingredients you decide to combine and simmer in your soup pot—may all your soups be lip-smackin' good. (And don't forget some crusty bread for dunking!)

Quick Vegetable Soup

about 4 servings

Taking the mystery out of making homemade soup in a snap is just one of the many tricks I have up my sleeve!

2 cans (10.5 ounces each) condensed chicken or beef broth
2 soup cans of water
3 cups frozen mixed vegetables or medium-diced fresh vegetables of your choice (such as carrots, peas, corn, etc.)
½ cup uncooked small pasta (such as orzo, ditalini, or acine di pepe)
1 tablespoon dried parsley flakes

In a medium-sized saucepan, combine the broth and water over high heat. Add the vegetables and bring to a boil. Stir in the pasta and parsley, then reduce the heat. Cover and simmer for 15 to 20 minutes, or until the vegetables and pasta are tender.

NOTE: You can even add some leftover cooked pasta instead of the ½ cup uncooked pasta. (About 1 cup cooked pasta will do.)

Time and Money Savers

- What about **leftover** spaghetti and sauce on an English muffin, **topped with** pepperoni and mozzarella cheese?
- Go exotic **and make** a Greek pizza: Put some thinly sliced cooked lamb **on** a pita bread and top with herb cheese.

After you **assemble** your creation, follow the cooking instructions **in** the following recipe.

Make Your Kitchen a Pizzeri[a]

Problem: It's late at night and you've got a cravin[g]. "No problem!" you think—till you find out that t[he] zeria is closed and you're out of frozen pizza. You['ve got] pizza "munchies" and you don't really want t[o go] without that pizza! No problem!

No More Pizza "Munchie[s"]

If a "traditional" pizza just can't be [had,] make your own. It's quick and easy. A[nd] be adventurous! Here are the basics:

- Start with a bread base. Use anything from Itali[an bread,] English muffins, bagels, or even pita bread.
- Next come the sauce and toppings. Traditional [is a] rich red sauce, but you can really get daring a[nd] unique. Toppings could be anything from cooke[d meats to] different kinds of cheese and veggies. But w[hy not try] these:
- Make a "pizza" of ham and Swiss cheese slice[s with mus-]tard on an English muffin.
- Scrambled eggs on a buttered bagel, topped wit[h] cheese and dill. It's a breakfast pizza!
- Spread some bottled pesto sauce on Italian br[ead] with sliced black olives and Muenster cheese.
- Try some chunks of tuna fish and tomatoes [with] Havarti cheese on pita bread for a gourmet-ty[pe pizza.]

Quick and Easy Pizza

8 slices

Quick pizza that you can make at home in minutes, and the options are limitless. Here are my traditional favorites...

4 bagels or English muffins, sliced in half
1 cup pizza or spaghetti sauce
1 cup (4 ounces) shredded mozzarella cheese

Preheat the oven to 350°F. Place the 8 bagel or English muffin halves on a cookie sheet, cut side up. Spread each with 2 tablespoons pizza sauce and top each with 2 tablespoons cheese. Bake for 15 minutes or until the cheese is melted.

NOTE: I recommend toasting or broiling the bagel or English muffin halves before adding the sauce and cheese. This helps keep the "crust" from getting soggy. Shredded mozzarella melts nicely, but you can use whatever cheese you have on hand—and it doesn't even have to be shredded. Here are more options:

- You can use pita pockets, too—but don't cut those in half. (Use 4 whole small pockets for this recipe.)
- Add your favorite toppings and, if you want, make them ahead and reheat them.
- If you want to make this just for yourself, then adjust the ingredient quantities and make as many as you'll eat (and use the toaster oven if it's easier!).

How to Get the Most from Fresh Strawberries

Problem: I betcha strawberries are one of the most popular fruits when it comes to fancying up a fruit platter or topping special desserts. But **they always seem to soften and bruise so quickly and easily.**

Keep Them "Berry Berry" Fresh

To keep strawberries fresher longer, I suggest these few quick storage tips:

- Do not wash strawberries until ready to use.
- Store strawberries in a single layer on a cookie sheet lined with paper towels. If any begin to get moldy, remove them immediately and discard them. (Mold is contagious, so spreading them out will keep any moldy ones from affecting the others.)
- To wash strawberries, run cold water gently over them, *then* remove the stems (or leave them on for extra garnishing color, if desired). Dry them by placing them in a single layer on paper towels.

After a while, ripened strawberries will begin to soften. Here are a few ways to use them once they've begun to soften:

- Clean the berries and remove the stems. Lay them out in a single layer on a cookie sheet. Freeze until solid, then place in airtight plastic bags and keep frozen for later use.
- Clean the berries and remove the stems. Place the berries

in a blender with some sugar, orange juice or water, and lots of ice for nonalcoholic strawberry daiquiris. Add a splash of rum and you'll have the traditional alcoholic version of this drink.
- Cut away the overripe part of the berries and discard. Slice up the still-good parts of the berries and sprinkle with sugar. This makes a great topping for pancakes or strawberry shortcake.
- Get out the canning equipment and begin creating super homemade jams and jellies.

Summer Strawberry Sauce

about 1½ cups

One of my favorite ways with strawberries is to make fresh strawberry sauce. It's the perfect addition to shortcake, pound cake, ice cream, or even over waffles and pancakes.

2 cups sliced fresh strawberries (about 1 pint)
1¾ cups water, divided
⅓ cup sugar
1 tablespoon cornstarch

Place the sliced strawberries in a medium-sized saucepan with 1½ cups water and the sugar. Cook over medium heat for 25 minutes, stirring occasionally. In a small bowl, mix the remaining ¼ cup water with the cornstarch and slowly add to the strawberry mixture. Reduce the heat to low and simmer for 5 to 8 minutes, or until slightly thickened.

NOTE: Add 1 or 2 drops of red food color to give the sauce a ruby-red finish.

Tips for Sprucing Up Packaged Food Mixes

Problem: I was invited to a potluck dinner last week, and I was asked to bring a dessert. Well, I had such a busy week that I almost forgot about the dinner! **I had only a couple of hours to put something together.** I thought about making a quick cake mix, but wasn't sure it would be the right thing to bring. **After all, how could I, MR. FOOD®, bring just a cake from a mix??**

"Mix It Up" with Mixes

Okay, I'll admit it . . . I did use a packaged cake mix—but wait till I tell you how I fancied it up: with mix-ins. I added some personal touches to make it my own "creation." When I walked into the dinner and set my dessert next to those other boxed cakes, I winked at my wife 'cause I had at least done something a little bit extra to give my dessert a special touch. You can do it, too—with lots of packaged foods. **The key is not to be afraid to experiment.**

- Try adding some fun mix-ins to your favorite boxed cake mix. Add chocolate chips to strawberry cake mix and call it Strawberry Watermelon Surprise. The surprise is the chocolate chips . . . they'll look like watermelon seeds in the red cake.
- Cut down on the amount of liquid in your cake mix to make the batter the consistency of drop cookie dough. Simply drop

continued

Time and Money Savers

them on a cookie sheet that has been coated with nonstick vegetable spray and bake until the edges are golden.

Cake mixes aren't the only mixes that can be spruced up. Other mixes can be customized, too:
- Biscuit baking mix certainly is quite popular. You can use it to make everything from pancakes to quick bread and rolls. And if you add a few mix-ins, everybody will think you started from scratch. (If you don't tell them, I sure won't!)
- Try adding beer to pancake mix to make a beer batter that's perfect for chicken or fish.
- Add fresh vegetables, chopped nuts, or leftover chunks of cooked meats to those convenience rice and noodle mixes to make store convenience the beginning of good old homemade.

Pineapple Upside-Down Cake

12 servings

A little creativity, a box of cake mix, and lots of everybody saying "It doesn't taste like cake mix!"...'cause it doesn't!

½ cup butter or margarine, melted and still warm
⅔ cup firmly packed light brown sugar
10 canned pineapple slices (from a 20-ounce can), drained
10 maraschino cherries, drained and halved
Prepared batter from 1 box (18.25 ounces) yellow cake mix

Preheat the oven to 350°F. In a small bowl, combine the melted butter and brown sugar. Stir until the sugar is mostly dissolved. Pour into the bottom of a 9" × 13" glass baking dish that has been coated with nonstick vegetable spray. Cut each pineapple slice in half and place the slices over the butter mixture. Place a cherry half in the center of each half-slice. Pour the cake batter over the pineapple halves. Bake for 35 to 40 minutes or until a wooden toothpick inserted in the center comes out clean. Let cool for 15 to 20 minutes, then invert onto a serving tray and serve warm, or allow to cool completely before serving.

Quick Deglazing

Problem: You just panfried some chicken, fish, or meat, and after removing it from the pan **you were left with a pan covered with crispy golden-brown tidbits of flavor stuck to it. What a mess!** Well, if you throw them away, it's almost like **pouring the best part down the drain!**

Fancy Sauce, Easy Cleanup

You know, **in fancy restaurants they use the pan drippings to make their best sauces.** You can do it, too. The process they use is called deglazing, but I prefer to call it "French glaze." Here's how it works:

- After sautéing or panfrying any fish, chicken, or meat, remove it from the pan and set aside.
- Drain and discard any oil remaining in the pan (but do not scrape or wipe out the pan).
- Return the pan to medium heat and add about ½ cup liquid to the pan. That could be lemon or other fruit juice, dry wine, or chicken or beef stock. Mix it around and simmer (cook over low heat) for 3 to 4 minutes while stirring frequently.

Almost as fast as you can say "Abracadabra!" those crispy tidbits that were once a cleanup headache are now the base of a fancy sauce. This is great for an all-in-one-pan quick sauce with little work—and it's economical 'cause you made it with the leftover flavor that normally gets poured down the drain.

French-Glazed Chicken

3 to 4 servings

Easy cleanup and lots of flavor—in the snap of a finger. Now that's my kind of recipe!

½ cup all-purpose flour
½ teaspoon salt
⅛ teaspoon white pepper
About ½ cup vegetable oil (enough to cover the bottom of a large skillet)
4 skinless and boneless chicken breast halves (1¼ to 1½ pounds), pounded to ⅓" to ½" thick and moistened with water

Glaze
3 tablespoons lemon juice
3 tablespoons dry white wine
2 tablespoons water
Dash of salt

In a medium-sized bowl, combine the flour, salt, and pepper. In a large skillet, heat the oil over medium-high heat. Dip each moistened chicken breast into the flour mixture, coating well on each side. Sauté the chicken until light golden on each side, about 7 minutes per side. Remove the chicken to a platter, reduce the heat to medium, and add the glaze ingredients to the pan, stirring constantly to loosen the browned bits from the bottom of the pan. When the sauce has thickened slightly, return the chicken to the pan and coat well. When the chicken is heated through, remove to the platter. Pour any remaining sauce over the top and serve immediately.

NOTE: With this sauce and a sprinkle of chopped fresh parsley over the whole dish, you'll think dinner was made by a gourmet chef!

What to Do with Cookie Crumbs

Problem: Every time I open a package of cookies, or whenever I make a batch of my favorites, **there always seem to be some broken ones. They're too good to throw away, but not pretty enough to serve to company.**

If the Cookie Crumbles...

Here are some great ways for these crumbs and pieces to have a glowing second life!

- Place the broken cookies in a plastic bag, seal, and roll with a rolling pin to crush everything to the same texture. Set aside for topping ice cream and puddings.
- Stir broken cookie pieces into slightly softened vanilla ice cream and make your own homemade Cookies and Cream ice cream.
- Stir chunks of broken cookies into a cake mix and bake the cake as directed. That's the answer to those times when you can't decide between cake and cookies!
- Decorate your iced desserts by sprinkling cookie crumbs over the icing. It's a super, fun look, plus the flavor is ooh-la-la!

Cookie Pie Crust

one 6- to 8-serving pie crust

The perfect solution is making your own cookie pie crust and filling it with your favorite pie filling. From crumbs to crust in just minutes!

1½ cups cookie crumbs (made from crisp types of cookies, such as butter cookies, chocolate and vanilla sandwich cookies, graham crackers, spice cookies, vanilla wafers, ginger snaps, or chocolate chip cookies)

¼ cup butter or margarine, melted

Preheat the oven to 350°F. Crush your favorite cookies by rolling them in a sealed plastic bag with a rolling pin, or in a food processor with a cutting blade, until a fine crumb mixture is formed. Place the crumbs in a medium-sized bowl and mix with the butter, blending well. Press into the bottom and sides of an 8- or 9-inch pie pan that has been coated with nonstick vegetable spray. Bake for 8 to 10 minutes, then cool. Fill with your favorite filling and refrigerate or freeze as the filling requires.

NOTE: Suggested fillings are ice cream, pudding, mousse, and canned pie filling. You can add several tablespoons of sugar to the cookie crumbs if you'd like a sweeter crust.

Better the Second Time Around

We've all heard the saying about enjoying things today because we "only go around once." Well, I want to take that a little further. Say you really enjoy tonight's dinner, and you end up with leftovers. Instead of throwing them out, why not enjoy your food today *and* enjoy it all over again—a new way—tomorrow?

I don't know why some people complain about eating leftovers, because I love them. Do you think it's because I make some really great stuff with leftovers? I guess if you didn't know what to do with them, then you might have a point. But if you knew you could make a great breakfast or lunch quiche with your leftover ham and cheese (page 163), or a yummy Oriental Pasta Salad with leftover spaghetti (page 160), maybe you'd change your mind!

And what about making an awesome Banana Bread (page 149) with your overripe bananas? Or a really different Coffee Gelatin (page 171) with leftover perked coffee?

The tips and recipes in this chapter will make a real difference in your food budget *and* in the variety of dishes you serve. You've got to give them a try—'cause when *these* leftovers go around the table a second time, no one will ever know these foods are getting a second chance!

Contents

Better the Second Time Around

What to Do with Leftovers	145
Recipe: Spicy Ham and Cheese Salad	146
Giving Ripe Bananas a Second Life	147
Recipe: Banana Bread	149
Using Leftover Cooked Potatoes	150
Recipe: All-in-One Breakfast	151
What to Do with Stale Bread	152
Recipes: Crispy Croutons	153
Quick Homemade Bread Crumbs	154
TV Dinners to Be Proud Of	155
Fun Ways with Leftover Pasta	158
Recipe: Oriental Pasta Salad	160
Ideas for Using Leftover Cheese	161
Recipe: Ham and Cheese Quiche	163

Better the Second Time Around

Using the Juice from Canned Fruit	164
Recipe: Fruity Marinated Chicken Breasts	165
Don't Throw Away That Leftover Pickle Juice	166
Recipe: "Pickle Me Silly" Tips	167
Using Stale Cakes to Make New Treats	168
Recipe: Fruit Trifle	169
New Life for Leftover Coffee	170
Recipe: Coffee Gelatin	171

What to Do with Leftovers

Problem: After the holidays and big family get-togethers, **we always seem to have a refrigerator full of leftover odds and ends. It never seems to be enough to serve the family, but we hate just throwing out all those bits and pieces that are still good!**

Looking Forward to Leftovers

There might not be enough of one item to serve the whole family, but before we throw away those stray veggies, lonely pieces of meat, and almost-empty condiment jars, we can **make creative salads** that combine a bit of several different ingredients. By mixing them together we can come up with some special new dishes. (Now that's what I call economical!)

- A little leftover plain pasta combined with yesterday's leftover cooked vegetables could be the beginning of a great pasta salad. Use your favorite recipe or make up a new one!
- Tidbits of cooked turkey, chicken, fish, and ham could be the hearty addition to a soup or stew.
- Potatoes, rice, and beans are great served cold with a splash of your favorite salad dressing, and you could even add some olives or pickles left over from your relish platter.
- Those few leftover slices of deli meat might be just the beginning of a yummy batch of hash.

Spicy Ham and Cheese Salad

4 to 6 servings

Turn leftovers into recipes that the family will ask for over and over. Leftovers never tasted so good!

- 2 cups small cooked ham chunks
- ¾ cup (3 ounces) shredded Cheddar cheese
- ⅓ cup chopped onion
- ¼ cup sweet pickle relish, drained
- ½ cup mayonnaise
- 1 tablespoon spicy brown mustard
- ¼ teaspoon black pepper

Place all ingredients in a food processor and process with a cutting blade on medium speed for 1 minute. Scrape down the sides of the bowl with a rubber spatula and process for another minute. Serve as a sandwich filling. And, served with crackers, it also makes a great appetizer spread!

NOTE: Why not try using leftover cooked turkey, chicken, or corned beef in place of the ham? The results will surely be just as awesome!

Giving Ripe Bananas a Second Life

Problem: But . . . but . . . I just bought these bananas a few days ago, and they're already brown and overripe. What should I do?!

"Apeeling" Banana Tips

The hotter it is, the quicker bananas ripen when left sitting out in your kitchen. Usually I recommend leaving them out on your kitchen counter, but if you want to slow down the natural ripening process, **store them in the refrigerator.** Yes, this will make their skins dark, but it won't change the edible insides at all (except to make them cold!).

When you do have leftover overripe bananas, don't worry:

- Make a rich, full-flavored milkshake by mixing 1 or 2 bananas in a blender with milk and ice cream until well combined.
- Freeze them in 1-inch slices; then you have them for adding to a milkshake whenever you want! The frozen banana "chips" chill the shake without diluting it like ice does.
- Stick a popsicle stick into the end of a peeled ripe banana and freeze it as explained below. Once frozen, dip the banana in chocolate fondue or melted chocolate chips, cover with waxed paper, and refreeze on waxed paper. Serve instead of a popsicle as a fun summertime (or anytime!) treat.

Here are some tips for freezing bananas:

- Peel bananas and leave whole. Place in plastic bags, seal, and freeze. They'll last this way for up to a month. (To keep

continued

Better the Second Time Around

them from sticking together, lay them out on a cookie sheet until frozen; then, when frozen, store in tightly sealed plastic bags.)
- If you prefer, peel bananas and purée in a food processor or blender until mashed. Freeze in plastic containers or empty whipped butter or margarine containers.
- Fresh-sliced or thawed and sliced bananas are great sautéed in a mixture of brown sugar and butter. Serve over ice cream, cake, or in individual graham cracker tart shells. (Check out Bananas Foster on page 7.)

Banana Bread

1 loaf

Banana bread and banana muffins sure give the best-tasting second life to overripe bananas that you could ever find! And if you have only a couple of bananas left (not enough to make this whole recipe)? Peel, mash, and freeze them. Then when you have more, just thaw the frozen ones and make everybody's favorite...

1 cup sugar
½ cup vegetable shortening
2 eggs
1 teaspoon baking soda
2 cups all-purpose flour
½ teaspoon salt
1 cup mashed bananas (about 3 ripe bananas)
1 teaspoon vanilla extract
½ cup chopped walnuts

Preheat the oven to 350°F. In a large bowl, cream together the sugar and shortening until light and fluffy. Add the eggs and beat thoroughly. Gradually blend in the baking soda, flour, and salt. Beat in the mashed bananas and vanilla until well mixed. Fold in the chopped walnuts. Pour the mixture into a 9" × 5" loaf pan that has been coated with nonstick vegetable spray. Bake for 50 to 55 minutes or until light golden. Remove from the pan immediately and place on a wire rack to cool.

NOTE: If you like it a bit sweeter, like I do, use an additional ¼ cup sugar. And if your gang likes muffins, just fill regular-sized greased muffin tins ¾ full with the batter and bake for 17 to 20 minutes or until light golden.

Using Leftover Cooked Potatoes

Problem: Didn't you have baked potatoes a few nights ago? Didn't you have a few left over? They're sitting in your fridge right now, so **how can you use them?**

Dig Out Those Potatoes... Again!

Why not use leftover baked potatoes to make another spud specialty?

- Hollow them out and make filled potato skins. Reserve the potato pulp for another use, then fill the skins as is or fry them. Then fill them with shredded cheese, sour cream and bacon, chili, applesauce, creamed soup, or fresh cooked veggies. Then broil, bake, or microwave until hot throughout.
- You can microwave the potatoes whole. Just rub a bit of water on the outsides and they'll be almost as good as they were the first time.
- You can peel and cut them for adding to soups, stews, and salads.
- You can dice and fry them in a little olive or vegetable oil for home fries, or sauté them with some chopped bell peppers and onions for quick Potatoes O'Brien.
- Cut potatoes into thick slices and brush with melted butter mixed with salt, pepper, and paprika. Grill for 5 to 8 minutes on the barbecue.

All-in-One Breakfast

4 to 6 servings

Why not cut up leftover potatoes for a recipe where they won't look like leftovers? Here's a favorite of mine. My family loves it when we have leftover potatoes, 'cause they know I'll be making them this all-in-one treat!

4 tablespoons butter or margarine
¾ cup chopped onions
½ cup chopped red or green bell pepper
2 boiled or baked potatoes, peeled and sliced
6 eggs
2 tablespoons milk
½ teaspoon salt
¼ teaspoon white pepper
⅓ cup grated Parmesan cheese (optional)

In a large skillet, heat the butter over medium heat. When melted and bubbling lightly, add the onions and bell pepper. Sauté for about 5 minutes until the onions are softened. Add the potatoes and sauté for about 10 minutes or until the mixture starts to brown. In a medium-sized bowl, beat the eggs with the milk, salt, and white pepper. Pour the egg mixture into the pan. Sprinkle with the Parmesan cheese, if desired. Stir gently until the eggs are set but not dry (about 8 to 10 minutes). Serve immediately.

What to Do with Stale Bread

Problem: Doesn't it annoy you when somebody in your family takes a piece of bread out of the package and forgets to close it back up? Before you get to it, the whole loaf is stale? It doesn't take long. Does it all have to be a waste? No way!

Not Just for the Birds Anymore

The next time this happens to you—as long as the bread is not fresh enough for anything else, but not yet rock hard—you can make the best of it by making any of these:

- **Bread pudding:** It's simply a baked mixture of stale bread cubes, milk, eggs, sugar, and cinnamon. It's a great use for old bread and rolls, so dig out your favorite recipe!
- **Toast:** Stale bread is great toasted. Maybe make a toasted sandwich. Or make toast points and serve your favorite cream-style dish (like Chicken à la King) over them.
- Stale rolls make great **garlic bread**, simply topped with a mixture of butter and garlic, then broiled.

Crispy Croutons

4 cups

When you have stale bread, croutons are a natural. Use any type of bread—white, rye, with or without seeds—and this quick recipe will make you a salad or soup hero with every crunch!

About 8 slices stale bread, cut into ½-inch chunks to make 4 cups
4 tablespoons butter or margarine, melted
1 teaspoon garlic powder
½ teaspoon salt
¼ teaspoon pepper

Preheat the oven to 375°F. Place the bread chunks into a medium-sized bowl. Combine the remaining ingredients in a small bowl. Lightly toss the bread chunks with the butter mixture and place on a large rimmed cookie sheet; bake for 20 minutes or until lightly browned and crunchy throughout. Let cool, then store in an airtight container until ready to use.

NOTE: Want cheesy croutons? Just add a tablespoon of grated Parmesan cheese along with the other seasonings.

Quick Homemade Bread Crumbs

about 2½ cups

It's easy to impress the gang with bread crumbs made from scratch. You'll never want to buy bread crumbs again!

2 slices stale bread or 1 large stale roll

For seasoned bread crumbs:
½ teaspoon garlic powder (optional)
1 teaspoon dried oregano
1 teaspoon dried parsley flakes
½ teaspoon salt

Grate the bread in a food processor or blender until the crumbs are fine. For seasoned bread crumbs, add the garlic powder, oregano, parsley, and salt to the fine bread crumbs and mix until thoroughly combined. Store in an airtight container until ready to use.

TV Dinners to Be Proud Of

Problem: The '60s and '70s were booming years for TV dinners. And why not? They were a great concept from even earlier that had really caught on because they fit into our busy, changing lifestyles. And even today, what could be better than buying a complete meal that you can keep frozen and have ready to eat in no time? Of course, frozen dinners have come a long way, but they still aren't the same as our own home cooking. Well, **wouldn't it be great to have your own homemade "TV dinners" in the freezer?** You can . . . and they'll have all the convenience and variety of store-bought frozen dinners.

Switch Channels to Homemade

The time has come to make your own TV dinners. Sure! Think about it—how many times do you have a portion of this and a little bit of that left over from dinner? **Those single portions are hardly worth saving by themselves, but you can put them together to make your own single-serve frozen dinners.** You can buy divided trays, in plastic or aluminum, in the housewares section of most supermarkets and discount stores. Plastic trays are great for microwaving, and aluminum ones are the answer for reheating your dinners in the oven. (You can even save the trays from store-bought frozen dinners and reuse them for your own frozen meals.) Before I

continued

share my list of favorite dinner combinations with you, here are some tips for storing your quick meals:

- Use only foods that freeze well—I wouldn't recommend freezing cooked steak, but turkey with gravy, and thinly sliced roast beef with mushroom or other sauce, are ideal.
- Always be certain that the food is cold before covering and freezing it. If it goes into the freezer hot, ice will form from the steam.
- Wrap the complete containers tightly with plastic wrap or aluminum foil. If your food gets freezer burned, it will be ruined.
- There is no need to thaw your dinner before heating. Keep the dinner loosely wrapped during heating. **(Remember to first remove any plastic wrap if heating in the oven, and any aluminum foil if heating in the microwave!)**
- An average dinner should be heated for about 30 to 40 minutes in a preheated 350°F. oven. Times may vary by portion size and type of food being heated.
- Cooking times also vary greatly from one microwave to the next, so if heating your dinner in the microwave (which can be done on high power), check and stir the food frequently, and cook until heated through.

Better the Second Time Around

Here are a few of my favorite combinations:

Main Dish	Vegetable	Starch
Turkey slices with gravy	Buttered peas	Stuffing or mashed potatoes
Sliced ham with raisin sauce	Baked apple slices	Biscuit
Thinly sliced roast beef with gravy	Cauliflower	Roasted red potatoes
Hot dog and baked bean casserole	Buttered corn	Garlic bread slices
Macaroni and cheese	Green beans	Not needed
Veal cutlet with extra sauce and mozzarella cheese	Broccoli florets	Spaghetti with sauce
Meat loaf and gravy	Butternut squash	Mashed potatoes

Fun Ways with Leftover Pasta

Problem: Talk about magic! Pasta just seems to multiply magically when you cook it! **So many of us cook up what looks like a reasonable amount for dinner, and then we have it left over.** Want to know what to do with it?

Endless "Pasta-bilities"

Some people think that pasta always gets covered with a tomato sauce—and that's it. Boy, are those people missing out! What *I* like about pasta is how versatile it is—and it's super when it's left over! Why not **make some magical creations by turning yesterday's macaroni into tomorrow's pasta specialty**? No more pasta down the drain!

When pasta is left over, just rinse it under cold water and drain. Then toss it with a light coating of vegetable oil, place in a dish, cover, and store in the refrigerator for up to 3 days.

Try any of these popular combinations tonight with your leftover plain (unsauced) pasta:

- Toss leftover cooked pasta with bottled or fresh pesto sauce and some chopped red bell peppers for a fancy pasta salad.
- With a little cheese and a few chunks of leftover meat, you've got the beginnings of a great casserole.
- Toss leftover small pasta shells with mayonnaise and add some real or imitation crabmeat and a squeeze of lemon... Presto! You have a fresh-tasting summer salad or super appetizer.

Better the Second Time Around

- Beef up leftover pasta by adding cooked ground meats, sauces (tomato or cream), and vegetables. These can be combined in a large skillet or in a casserole dish and topped with cheese before baking.
- A cupful of leftover pasta is the perfect addition to almost any soup (except cream soups). But be careful not to add too much because it absorbs liquid and swells. (See Yes, You Can! page 126.)
- Why not add leftover pasta to your favorite vegetables, have it cold in salads, or stir-fry it? WOW!

Oriental Pasta Salad

4 to 6 servings

¼ cup vegetable oil
4½ teaspoons lemon juice
2 tablespoons soy sauce
⅛ teaspoon black pepper
1 to 2 cloves garlic, crushed
2 cups cold cooked spaghetti or linguine (about 8 ounces)
¾ cup thin angle-sliced scallions (about 2 scallions)

In a small bowl, combine the oil, lemon juice, soy sauce, pepper, and garlic. Add the spaghetti and toss to coat. Top the spaghetti with the scallions and serve.

NOTE: For some extra crunch, add ½ cup sliced and drained canned water chestnuts.

Ideas for Using Leftover Cheese

Problem: You open your refrigerator and look on your door or in your cheese section. You find a chunk of *this* cheese and a small piece of *that* cheese. Maybe you remember putting them in there, but you never got back to finishing them. You looked at them a few times, but decided to wait on them, and instead you started a fresh package. After all, don't they say that cheese is better aged? **You guess you'll use it some other time . . . you know, "later"—but how?**

Bits and Pieces Can Make You "The Big Cheese"

Cheese sure is better when it is aged, but that doesn't mean spoiled! Even if your cheese has a bit of mold growing on it, it doesn't always mean that it has to end up in the garbage! Simply trim off the mold and discard it. Then, as long as the remaining cheese is still good, use it in a recipe. Cheese is so versatile that I could list hundreds of uses, but here are a few tips to help you cook with it:

- Toss a cup of shredded cheese into soups or cream sauces and watch them come alive. Just grate it first and stir it into warmed soups or sauces.
- Use strong-flavored cheeses more sparingly than mild ones, 'cause you don't want to cover all the other flavors in your dish.
- Use low to moderate temperatures when preparing cheese dishes. Too high a heat will produce a rubbery, chewy tex-

continued

Better the Second Time Around

ture. This will happen, too, if you cook the cheese for too long.

Some of my favorite uses for cheese are:
- Topping casseroles with cheese slices and baking until melted. Usually, you only need to add the cheese topping to a casserole during the last 10 minutes of cooking time.
- Covering a crusty French bread with garlic or herb butter and fresh vegetables, then topping with sliced or shredded mozzarella or Havarti cheese and broiling or baking until the cheese melts.
- Serving a wedge of cheese with fresh fruit for a refreshing snack or dessert.

Ham and Cheese Quiche

6 to 8 servings

Ham and cheese are a perfect combination. So they're naturals sandwiched into a pie shell to become a gangbuster quiche.

- 1 cup (4 ounces) shredded Swiss cheese
- 1 9-inch frozen pie shell, thawed
- 1½ cups cooked ham chunks
- 1 cup (4 ounces) shredded Cheddar cheese
- 2 eggs, beaten
- ½ pint heavy cream

Preheat the oven to 350°F. Place the Swiss cheese in the pie shell, then top it with the ham, then the Cheddar cheese. In a small bowl, combine the eggs and the heavy cream and pour evenly over the top. Bake for 30 to 35 minutes or until the center is set. Cool for 10 minutes before serving.

NOTE: Swiss and Cheddar cheeses are traditional for quiche, but you could certainly use a combination of whatever kinds you've got left over. You could start a tradition of having a different flavor combination every time you make it!

Using the Juice from Canned Fruit

Problem: So often we'll open a can of sliced peaches or fruit cocktail and have the fruit for a snack, or use it in a recipe. But we're usually left with a good amount of fruit juice in the can. It sure is a waste to pour it all out. After all, we've paid for it, so why shouldn't we enjoy it *all*? How can we do that?

New Uses for Fruit Juices

Boy, I hate to waste anything, so I had to figure out a use for all that excess canned fruit juice. Here are a few of my suggestions that will make yesterday's "down the drain" into tomorrow's favorites—and with hardly any work:

- Freeze leftover fruit juice in ice cube trays for a fruit-flavored addition to any drink or punch.
- Add it to gelatin in place of water to make your dessert extra fruity.
- By adding this fruit juice to a cake mix in place of the liquid specified in the package directions, you add to both the flavor and the moistness of the cake.
- Use it for sweetening and moistening trifles (page 168).
- A couple of tablespoons added to bottled salad dressing gives your salad topper a fruity pick-me-up.

Fruity Marinated Chicken Breasts

4 servings

They say when life gives us lemons we should make lemonade. So I guess that means when life gives us fruit juice, we should give it another life—and here's an easy way that you'll really enjoy!

½ cup pineapple juice from a 20-ounce can of pineapple (any style)
¼ cup Italian dressing

4 skinless and boneless chicken breast halves (1 to 1¼ pounds)

In a medium-sized bowl, combine the pineapple juice and Italian dressing. Place the chicken in the mixture, cover, and marinate in the refrigerator for 2 to 3 hours or overnight. Preheat the barbecue grill to medium-high. Remove the chicken from the marinade, discarding any excess marinade. Place the chicken halves on the rack about 6 inches from the heat for 12 to 18 minutes, turning occasionally, or until the chicken is cooked through and no pink remains.

NOTE: This will also work well with French dressing instead of Italian. And if you want to broil the chicken instead of grilling it, that'll work, too (and for the same amount of cooking time).

Don't Throw Away That Leftover Pickle Juice

Problem: Open up your refrigerator and you'll probably find 2 or 3 jars of pickles in there with maybe only 1 or 2 lonely pickles floating in each jar. I don't know if everyone is being polite and not eating the last pickle, or if maybe there's some superstition about eating the last pickle that I just haven't heard of! And of course, when you really have the taste for pickles and you reach in and find just one left, then you get upset 'cause you don't want to eat the last one and be the one who has to pour out the pickle juice (the brine). **Why not stretch the goodness?**

Triple Your Pickles

I found a great solution that will leave you with a refrigerator full of pickles *and* save you money, too! When your pickle jar is nothing but pickle juice, slice cucumbers into ¼-inch-thick pieces and put them right into the leftover brine, packing them tightly and filling the jar. Shake to cover the cucumbers and put them back into the refrigerator for 24 hours. Then you can begin eating your homemade "pickles." Now that's what I call quick! And when those are gone you can do it again. (I usually don't recommend making more than 2 extra batches of new "pickles" before finally pouring the juice out.)

"Pickle Me Silly" Tips

Do the same with these as explained on the previous page. It's an easy way to have your own homemade quick pickled veggies—in just a day:

- Add small cauliflower florets to the brine of sweet mixed pickles.
- Cut your cucumbers into 1-inch cubes for chunky pickle pieces.
- Add some thinly sliced onions to the pickle juice for pickled onions.
- Use the juice from any pickles—sweet pickles, sour, half-sour, bread and butters—the choice is yours!

Using Stale Cakes to Make New Treats

Problem: It happens all the time—the whole gang sings "Happy Birthday," you blow out the candles, serve the cake, and after everybody leaves, **there's still half a cake left!** Or you buy a pound cake, eat a few slices, and by the time you get back to it, **it's kind of stale.** But **you hate to just throw it out!** So don't! Make your next dessert a "trifle" better!

"Stale Mates"

Use your leftover dessert or birthday cake to make an all-new dessert: Trifle. I've done it lots of times, so believe me when I tell you that your guests will eat it and love it. The trick is to cut up your leftover cake and layer it in a serving bowl with pudding, mousse, gelatin, fresh or canned fruit and fruit juices, nuts, chocolate chips, flaked coconut, and even crumbled cookies—whatever you've got!

(And it sure is super topped with whipped cream or whipped topping!) The result is a torte that blends the dry cake with the moist add-ins. It makes dessert time more than a "trifle" special!

168

Fruit Trifle

6 to 8 servings

Use angel food cake, pound cake, iced cake, or a combination! Make trifle whenever you have leftover cake (or even doughnuts or danish!). You can change it every time you make it, by changing the fruit, pudding, and of course, the leftover cake!

2 cups milk
1 package (4-serving size) instant vanilla pudding and pie filling
5 cups cake cubes
1 can (16 ounces) sliced or diced peaches, drained and juice reserved
1 can (8 ounces) pineapple chunks or tidbits, drained and juice reserved
1½ cups whipped cream or whipped topping

In a medium-sized bowl, combine the milk and pudding mix. Mix with a wire whisk for 1 to 2 minutes, until thickened; set aside. In a medium-sized serving bowl, layer half the cake cubes, half the peaches and half the pineapple, then half the pudding. Repeat the layers, finishing with the remaining pudding. Top with the whipped cream. Cover and refrigerate until ready to serve.

NOTE: This is a fancy dessert that's easy to make—and it looks even fancier if you layer it in a trifle dish or other glass bowl, showing off the layers of different colors and ingredients! If you'd like, go ahead and garnish the top with fresh or canned fruit, cookie crumbs (page 140), or toasted nuts (page 186).

New Life for Leftover Coffee

Problem: How come it's always so hard to make the right amount of coffee? Well, guess what?! I've got a couple of ways to use the leftovers—and they'll have you *planning* to make extra coffee from now on!

"Perk Up" a Second Time

It's such a shame to waste leftover coffee. So let me share a couple of tips for "perking up" those leftover cups of java into a coffee lover's dream come true:

- **Pour leftover coffee into ice cube trays and freeze.** The cubes are the perfect way to cool down your hot coffee—1 or 2 will do the trick without watering it down.
- **Try coffee as the base of a fancy dessert.** It's easy to turn leftover coffee and unflavored gelatin into your own espresso version of a gelatin treat! (Check out the following recipe.)

Coffee Gelatin

4 servings

3 cups coffee, divided (1 cup cold, 2 cups hot)
2 envelopes (¼ ounce each) unflavored gelatin
4 tablespoons sugar
½ cup milk
Whipped cream or whipped topping (optional)
Ground cinnamon for sprinkling (optional)

Place the 1 cup cold coffee in a medium-sized bowl; sprinkle the gelatin over the coffee and let stand for 1 minute. Add the hot coffee, sugar, and milk, and stir until mixed. Pour into a 1-quart gelatin mold or a large serving bowl. Refrigerate for 3 hours or overnight, then top with the whipped cream and cinnamon before serving, if desired.

NOTE: To create a "hoo hoo fancy" coffee treat, maybe add a tablespoon of your favorite liqueur when you add the milk. And if you want to get really fancy, why not make this in individual-sized wine or parfait glasses?

> **TIP** Now that you've got a couple of new ways to use your leftover coffee, I can't forget to tell you this one: **Don't waste used coffee grounds. Add them to your garden.** (No, you won't grow your own coffee, but you *will* enrich the soil!)

The Frills

Okay, I've shared my tips for organizing your kitchen, saving time and money, and using leftovers, and I've even let you in on secrets for things that "you wish you knew before." Now it's time just to have fun in the kitchen!

I'll show you how to make delicious snacks from whatever you've got in your cupboards (page 191), make your foods more colorful and fun (page 175), and even how to make your kitchen into the best ice cream parlor in the neighborhood (page 180)!

But before you get started, why not create a new hot drink for yourself (page 194) and, of course, top it with a dollop of homemade whipped cream (page 198)? Oh, I guess that *is* a start. Well, now you've got the picture. This chapter is full of hints for having all-new cooking adventures. (And I have a feeling they're all gonna end with **"OOH it's so GOOD!!**™**"**)

Contents

The Frills

Making Meals Special with Color and Creativity	175
Recipe: Orange Blossom Surprises	179
The Best Toppings Are Right at Home!	180
Recipe: Chocolate Sundae Sauce	182
Making the Most of Ice	183
Recipe: Flavor-Packed Fruit Punch	185
Giving Nuts and Seeds Extra Flavor and Crunch	186
Recipe: Nutty Green Beans	188
Flavored Milk They Can't Refuse!	189
Recipe: Frozen Rocky Road Sandwiches	190
Create Your Own Snack Mixes	191
Recipes: Hodgepodge Snack	192
Awesome Munchies	193

The Frills

Flavor Your Hot Drinks	194
Recipes: Irish Coffee	196
Zesty Butterscotch Tea	196
Chocolate Mint Sipper	196
Real Whipped Cream All the Time!	197
Recipes: Real Whipped Cream Dollops	198
Steaming Mocha Cocoa	199

Making Meals Special with Color and Creativity

Problem: **Is there someone in your circle of friends who always has to outdo everyone else with fancy spreads?** Well, I'll tell you a secret—those fancy-looking garnishes and beautifully displayed dishes don't have to take lots of time, money, and work. Uh-uh. Try some of these easy tips and before you know it, *you'll* be the hit of the party circuit!

"Palette-able" Possibilities

Remember the expression about eating with your eyes as well as your mouth? It's true, but you don't have to "go to town" decorating your dishes. You can have fun dressing them up and, at the same time, making them more fun for your guests! How do you make sure your food looks appetizing?

- **Add color to your cooking.** No, not with paint! With creativity. Even if you don't think you're the creative type, it can be easy. Add some chopped red bell pepper to plain-looking potato salad. Try some sliced black olives in your fettuccine with cream sauce. Even your green salads can look alive if you add a variety of colorful veggie toppers. And for topping bland-looking roast beef? Try some scallion rings.
- **Shapes, shapes, shapes!** Sure, you always expect certain foods to be cut certain ways. Well, watch your gang's reactions if you make hamburgers in the shape of hot dogs, or

continued

The Frills

cut your salad tomatoes into small cubes for a new look! Try mixing several shapes and colors of pasta together (but they should all be about the same size so they'll cook in the same amount of time). It'll fancy-up your meal. Or maybe serve white pasta on one side of the plates and green (spinach) pasta on the other. When you add your red sauce you've got the colors of the Italian flag!

- **Serve food in unique containers.** No, you don't have to go out and buy expensive new serving dishes. Just look around your house for the dishes that you hardly ever use. How 'bout the turkey platter that comes out only on Thanksgiving? You can use that more often. And why not serve ice cream or pudding out of wine glasses for a change?! Now, that's an easy "special." Once I even put spaghetti in a sundae glass and topped it with a meatball (you know, like the cherry on top of a sundae)! Boy, did that get me cheers of appreciation!

- **Or how 'bout serving food out of edible containers?** It's pretty easy to hollow out a watermelon, shape it like a basket (with or without a handle), and fill it with whole or cut fresh fruit. It's even easier to split a cantaloupe in half, remove the seeds, and fill it with chicken or tuna salad. Another easy one is to scoop the pulp out of a whole tomato and fill it with cooked rice or vegetables. And one of my favorites is to use whole and cut fruit as an edible table centerpiece! It'll look even prettier dotted with fresh strawberries, too.

- **Get out of a rut!** Don't always make the same food the same way. If Wednesday is Pasta Day, then one week serve it with red sauce, the next with a cream sauce. Or if they're used to steak made on the grill, then make beef stew the next time. Adding some variety to your meal lineup sure is a nice way to show you care.

The Frills

Here's a list of some ingredients that can be the finishing touch for your mealtime masterpieces. This is just to get you started—experiment for yourself and I'm sure you'll come up with even more:

Greens: Highlight your food by lining a platter with any type of flat greens, from endive and escarole to leaf, romaine, and iceberg lettuce. For example, serve your pasta salad on a bed of romaine, or your Italian tomato salad in an iceberg leaf. It sort of makes a serving "cup" for salads.

Parsley: Chop it in the food processor or by hand and sprinkle it on foods for a fresh look and taste. It's even easier to put a few sprigs on or around your food. (And it's a natural breath freshener, too!)

Bell peppers: With green, red, yellow, orange, and purple ones widely available now, they're an easy way to add color to your foods. Just chop them for adding to foods, or cut them into rings and place them around finished dishes.

Scallions (green onions): A few whole, cleaned scallions on the side of a platter say "garden fresh." And why not chop them on an angle and use them for topping stir-fries and other dishes, giving them an Oriental flair?

Cherry tomatoes: Talk about simple! Brighten up your serving platters or individual plates by placing a few whole or halved cherry tomatoes here and there.

Fruit: The options are endless! Why not fancy-up your meals by adding a slice, wedge, or half of a lemon, lime,

continued

The Frills

orange, or grapefruit for flavor and color? And try placing a bunch of grapes on your cheese board.

Fruits and vegetables have color, and color is the key to garnishing. Just as an artist uses color on his canvas, you can pretend that your plates are your canvas and use colored foods as your palette for making all your future meals palatable!

Orange Blossom Surprises

4 servings

If you like oranges, then this citrus delight is for you... and the bowl you serve it in is as unique as the recipe! (It's really flavor-packed gelatin made in oranges, so don't let the directions scare you!)

1 package (4-serving size) orange gelatin dessert mix
1 cup boiling water
4 medium to large oranges
Cold water
8 maraschino cherries, chopped

In a medium-sized bowl, combine the gelatin mix and the boiling water. Mix well until the gelatin completely dissolves. Set aside. Slice each orange about ¾" from the top, reserving the tops. With a teaspoon, carefully scoop out the inside (the pulp) of each orange and reserve the shells. Place the pulp in a colander and drain the juice into a measuring cup. Separate the orange pieces from the white pith, discarding the pith and placing the pulp in the gelatin. When the juice is fully drained, add cold water to it to measure 1 cup, then add it to the gelatin mixture and stir well. Divide the chopped cherries evenly among the 4 orange shells. Divide the gelatin-orange mixture evenly among the orange shells. Place the tops back on the oranges. Refrigerate for 3 to 4 hours or until the gelatin is set.

NOTE: To make removing the inside of the oranges easier, after slicing off the orange tops, run a serrated knife or a grapefruit knife between the skins and the insides, making sure not to puncture the skins.

The Best Toppings Are Right at Home!

Problem: A lot of times when the whole family gets together and the subject of dessert comes up, they can never agree on what to have. Someone wants chocolate, others, strawberries. No, no—the kids feel like something sweet and gooey, like sticky caramel sauce! So, **how can you satisfy all those taste buds without making 10 different desserts?**

Why Go Out for Ice Cream?

If your family is like mine, then the answer to putting smiles on all those faces is easy: It's ice cream! That's it! Do I mean that you should take everybody out for ice cream? No, better (and cheaper) is to put together a **make-your-own-sundae bar.** You probably have all the ingredients right in the house already. Sure, you need the ice cream, but that's easy to pick up. And, with a little imagination, you can give the corner ice cream parlor a run for its money!

- First choose your **ice cream.** Any flavor will do, but I suggest either vanilla or chocolate, because it's better to start basic and build from there.
- You'll need a **sauce** to be the focal point of your scooped creation. No problem! Whip up a batch of chocolate sauce and serve it warm. (It's my personal favorite, and the recipe is on page 182!) You can also top your ice cream with bottled hot fudge, butterscotch topping, strawberry sauce (page 134), marshmallow creme, or crushed pineapple.

The Frills

- Next comes the best part, the real treats, the **sparkle-on-the-top** part. It can be the little bit of flaked coconut that's been in your cupboard, maybe toasted, or a few chopped nuts left over from last week's football bash, or even some crushed cookies or candy bars that you've got on hand already. Of course, your refrigerator will be a great place to look for toppings, too. Why not use up the maraschino cherries that just seem to keep moving from one side of the fridge to the other? Or a bit of fruit preserves or jam? Warmed slightly, they make a flavorful addition. And don't forget the whipped cream (page 198), or a spoonful of whipped topping!
- Adults may want to add a splash of liqueur to their sundaes like so many of the fancy restaurants do. Maybe crème de menthe or coffee liqueur (that would be like dessert and coffee in one bowl!)

The combinations are endless, so go through your pantry, freezer, and fridge, and find all sorts of ice cream toppings that will gather everybody around the dessert table and bring **"OOH it's so GOOD!!**™**"** smiles to their sticky lips!

Chocolate Sundae Sauce

3 cups

2 cups sugar
¾ cup baking cocoa
¼ cup all-purpose flour
¼ teaspoon salt

2 cups water
1 tablespoon vanilla extract
2 tablespoons butter

In a small bowl, combine the sugar, cocoa, flour, and salt; mix well. In a medium-sized saucepan, over medium heat, heat the water, vanilla, and butter until the butter melts. Add the sugar mixture and continue heating until the mixture is almost boiling and slightly thickened, stirring occasionally. Remove from the heat, cool slightly, and serve immediately, or store, covered, in the refrigerator for up to 3 weeks.

Making the Most of Ice

Situation: A friend of mine was putting the ice cubes into the punch at a party several years back, and I said, "Let me tell you a thing or two about ice." He thought I was kidding. After all, he'd been making ice cubes all his life—and he couldn't imagine what kind of ice advice I could possibly give him! **Ice is just frozen water, right? Well, that's not necessarily true!**

I Only Have "Ice" for You!

Here are a few ice hints:
- To make crystal-clear ice cubes, boil the water, then let it cool before placing it in your regular ice cube trays.
- After ice cubes are frozen solid, pop them out, place them in a plastic bag, and seal tightly. That way your ice shouldn't pick up odors and tastes from your freezer.
- When going away for more than a few days, leave a plastic sandwich bag of ice cubes in the freezer. If the power goes off for a period of time, then goes back on before you return, you'll know about it because the ice will have melted into one big blob, letting you know to check for spoilage in your fridge and freezer.
- Make ice molds in plastic containers, cleaned milk cartons, or gelatin molds to add to punch. Jazz up your drinks by adding flavor and colorful "pick-me-ups" to the ice molds—like maraschino cherries (juice and all), or maybe twists of lemon. And the grapes that fall off the

continued

The Frills

bunch into the bag? Add those to your ice molds, too, to fancy them up. Ice molds melt slowly, so punches stay colder for longer. And less ice means less water in the punch—no more diluted, watery-tasting punch. I bet you'll be an entertaining hero in no time.

Flavor-Packed Fruit Punch

about 2 quarts

Regular fruit juice and the juice from canned fruit are perfect for adding to ice cubes and ice molds. This punch is really flavorful when you use ice cubes made with the juice from canned peaches!

1 can (12 ounces) frozen orange juice concentrate, thawed
2 cups pineapple juice
24 ounces (2 12-ounce cans) lemon-lime–flavored soda
12 ice cubes or 1 1-quart ice mold

Combine the orange juice concentrate and pineapple juice in a punch bowl or large container. Just before serving, add the soda and ice cubes or ice mold. (If not serving right away, cover and refrigerate the mixture, and add the soda and ice just before serving.)

NOTE: You could use almost any flavor fruit juice and flavored ice cubes. Use your favorites!

Giving Nuts and Seeds Extra Flavor and Crunch

Problem: So many times people cook or bake with nuts or seeds and wonder why they have little or no taste. I know how that is, 'cause a while back my daughter was cooking for the holidays and decided to jazz up the vegetables a bit... you know, make them a bit more special. So she threw a couple of tablespoons of sliced almonds on top. My family thought they looked good, but when they tasted them, I think they were a bit disappointed. Then I tried them and realized **the nuts had little flavor (and were even a bit stale!).** I told her there was an easy way to add nuts to foods and have them taste good!

Toast 'Em, Roast 'Em, Eat 'Em Up

Here's what she learned: **To bring out the full flavor in nuts or seeds, you should toast them.** Toasting will not only bring out the taste but will crisp up nuts that may be on their way to going stale.
- To toast nuts or seeds: Spread them out on a cookie sheet and put them in a preheated 300°F. oven until lightly toasted or golden. This will vary from 5 to 10 minutes for seeds to 1 hour for large shelled nuts, so keep an eye on them. Once they start to brown, they're practically done. And if you want the nuts to have an even richer taste, drizzle a few teaspoons of butter over them and add a light sprinkle of salt just after removing them from the oven. Mmm! Now, that's flavor!

The Frills

- Another method is to deep-fry the nuts or seeds in a cup or so of oil at 350°F. until light pale in color. Line a cookie sheet with paper towels, then remove the nuts from the oil and drain the excess oil. Don't overcook them because they'll continue to cook even after they're removed from the oil.
- One other way to bring out the flavor is to cook the nuts or seeds in a skillet with a few tablespoons of oil or butter.

Nutty Green Beans

5 servings

Nutty? You betcha! The gang will go nutty for the big, nutty flavor in this recipe.

2 cups water
1 bag (16 ounces) frozen green beans
1 tablespoon butter or margarine
½ cup sliced almonds
¼ teaspoon salt

Place the water in a medium-sized saucepan and bring to a boil. Cook the frozen beans in the boiling water for 8 minutes, or until tender; drain the beans, then return them to the saucepan. In a small skillet, over medium heat, melt the butter and toast the almonds for 3 to 5 minutes or until golden brown. Remove from the heat. Add the almonds and the salt to the beans and stir until evenly coated. Serve immediately, or transfer to a casserole dish, cover, and hold for up to 30 minutes in a warm oven.

Flavored Milk They Can't Refuse!

Problem: My granddaughters love to drink juice. **All I ever hear is "Juice, juice, juice," but their mom wants them to drink milk, too** (you know, so our little ones will grow strong, healthy bones and whiter teeth)—but they just don't like the taste.

Milking It for All It's Worth

I'm a milk lover, so it's hard to believe that anybody doesn't like the taste of plain milk. But my secrets will make drinking milk fun and delicious for the non–milk lovers. And for those of us who already like milk . . . we'll *really* enjoy these fun ways with our old favorite:

- **Add flavors** like chocolate sauce or fresh strawberries to cold milk and mix in the blender.
- Make full-blown **milkshakes** by following the directions in the tip above, but adding a scoop or two of ice cream. Milkshakes are perfect for special occasions or even as a super pick-me-up snack.
- Here's my favorite: **"Moo" Juicers**! They're made like this: Pour 1 can (any size) of your favorite-flavor frozen juice concentrate into a large pitcher or jar. Add 3 juice cans of cold milk and stir or shake until well mixed. Serve immediately and watch the smiles appear! I bet after they hear the name they'll yell for "MOO-re!"

Frozen Rocky Road Sandwiches

30 sandwiches

It's a cookie—no, no—it's a pudding—no! Maybe a candy...? I guess it doesn't matter what you call it. It's a guaranteed snack-time favorite!

1 cup milk
1 package (4-serving size) instant chocolate pudding and pie filling
1 container (12 ounces) frozen whipped topping, thawed
1½ cups miniature marshmallows
1 cup miniature semisweet chocolate chips
¾ cup chopped peanuts
1 box (16 ounces) graham crackers

In a large bowl, combine the milk and pudding and beat with a wire whisk for 1 to 2 minutes. Stir in the whipped topping, marshmallows, chocolate chips, and peanuts. Split the graham crackers in half and lay out half of the crackers on each of 2 10" × 15" cookie sheets. Spread about 2 tablespoons of the pudding mixture on each graham cracker. Top with the remaining graham crackers, forming sandwiches, and lightly press each "sandwich" together. Cover with plastic wrap and freeze for about 2 hours. Then wrap each one individually and return to the freezer. Before serving, remove the sandwiches from the freezer and let stand for about 5 minutes to soften slightly.

Create Your Own Snack Mixes

Problem: How often do you get a phone call on a Sunday afternoon and find out that your buddies are on their way over? Well, they're going to want something to nibble on, so what can you throw together in a few minutes?

Mix 'Em, Match 'Em

Say good-bye to boring snacks and hello to **signature munchies**. I mean, **something that you put together with what you've got on hand.** Maybe toss a partial can of peanuts with a few Chinese noodles and chocolate chips. The combination sure will be memorable! Why not mix some dry cold cereal with some spicy seasonings to create a Tex-Mex delight? I think if you search your kitchen cupboards, you'll discover more variety than you ever thought you had! Make your own combination of nuts, cereals, chocolates, dried noodles, fried onions, popcorn, pretzels, cheese puffs, even broken crackers and bread sticks. Toss them with some spices and a little melted butter—a tablespoon or so per cup of mixture. Go Italian by adding basil and oregano, or Mexican with some dry taco seasoning. Maybe go hot and sour by adding a bit of sugar and a little hot pepper sauce to the melted butter. Now you know what I mean—mix 'em, match 'em, and drive their taste buds wild!

Hodgepodge Snack

7 cups

So sweet and crunchy, you'd better make a double batch! Make it ahead and keep 'em on hand in case company drops by.

2 cups oven-toasted corn cereal
2 cups oven-toasted rice cereal
1 cup honey-roasted peanuts
¼ cup (½ stick) butter or margarine
¼ cup sugar
1 cup chocolate-covered raisins

Preheat the oven to 350°F. In a large bowl, combine the cereals and peanuts. In a small saucepan, melt the butter over low heat and mix in the sugar until just dissolved. Pour the butter-sugar mixture over the cereal mixture; mix well to completely coat the cereal. Place on a large rimmed cookie sheet that has been coated with nonstick vegetable spray. Bake for 10 minutes. Remove from the oven and let cool completely (about 45 minutes to an hour). Place in a serving bowl and mix in the chocolate-covered raisins.

Awesome Munchies

8 cups

Next time you need a fun snack, just get the gang ready for some of your "Awesome Munchies"!

5 cups oven-toasted rice cereal
1 cup pretzel sticks
1 cup peanuts
1 cup cheese crackers
¼ cup (½ stick) melted butter or margarine, slightly cooled
3 tablespoons steak sauce
¼ teaspoon salt

Preheat the oven to 350°F. In a large bowl, combine the cereal, pretzels, peanuts, and crackers, then place in a large resealable plastic bag. Combine the remaining ingredients in a small bowl, then pour into the cereal mixture and shake until the cereal is evenly coated. Pour onto a large rimmed cookie sheet that has been coated with nonstick vegetable spray and bake for 10 minutes. Cool and serve.

NOTE: You can heat the mixture in the microwave for 5 to 6 minutes instead of baking it.

Flavor Your Hot Drinks

Problem: When your friends come over for the evening, do you always get a ton of requests, all for different hot drinks? Somebody wants coffee with a splash of chocolate liqueur, another wants cinnamon tea, and somebody else wants hot chocolate with mint. I've got easy ways to satisfy them all!

Sizzling Sippers

Sure, we can walk down the coffee aisle at the grocery store and be wowed by all the choices. I have a hint that will make your whole gang happy, and you don't have to stock up on all the gourmet-flavored mixes as long as you keep the basics on hand. I mean coffee, tea, and hot chocolate. Then you can just add in everybody's favorite flavors from items that you can always keep on hand. I'll share some tricks for adding zip to your sips:

- Add a few drops of food flavoring (they're called extracts) to your hot drinks. Try orange in tea, peppermint in hot chocolate, and butter in warm egg nog. They're really super and they're available in the supermarket spice department.
- Combine ¼ teaspoon ground spice with a teaspoon of sugar (and, of course, more if you'd like), and mix it into your hot drink. (In order for the spice to dissolve it must be mixed with the sugar first.) Try ground cinnamon, nutmeg, or even ginger.
- A fancy alternative would be to add some liqueur to adults' drinks. Coffee liqueur brings out the rich flavor of coffee,

The Frills

anisette adds a hint of licorice, and a touch of brandy or fruit-flavored liqueur can give your coffee a tropical pickup.

- I think some of the best additions to hot beverages are items that add flavor as they melt. For instance, try adding a piece of chocolate candy bar, some rock candy, or a butterscotch hard candy, and stir until it dissolves. With every stir comes another burst of pizzazz! **Just be sure to melt the candy completely or remove any unmelted pieces before drinking, so that they aren't swallowed whole!**
- And we even have a large choice of sugars! Be creative in sweetening the sips for the lips! Of course, granulated white sugar works fine, but why not offer extra-fine granulated sugar (which melts really easily), brown sugar, maple syrup, or honey. There are some fun sugars on the market, too, like colored granulated "crystal" sugars, coarse "raw" sugar, and good old sugar cubes.
- Oh, yes—don't forget the whipped cream! A dollop will be just fine (page 198), or else use some prepared whipped topping.

Flavored Hot Drinks

1 cup

Adding a little of this and a little of that will make your hot drinks burst with flavor! Try these:

Irish Coffee

To 1 cup of strong hot coffee add:

1 tablespoon Irish whiskey
1 tablespoon sugar

1 tablespoon cream or milk

Zesty Butterscotch Tea

To 1 cup of hot tea add:

2 butterscotch hard candies
1 tablespoon honey
½ teaspoon lemon juice
1 cinnamon stick

Stir until candies melt, or remove any remaining pieces before drinking.

Chocolate Mint Sipper

To 1 cup of hot chocolate (or 1 single-serving packet) add:

¼ teaspoon mint extract
1 tablespoon semisweet chocolate chips

15 miniature or 3 large marshmallows

Real Whipped Cream All the Time!

Problem: Just the mention of real whipped cream usually brings lots of smiles and even more "Ooh"s and "Ahh"s. But **how often do most of us actually stop and make our own?** Sure, we've got some good frozen whipped toppings and aerosol whipped creams available, but **why don't we make it ourselves more often? Think it's too hard? Only need a little?**

Dollops for Days

Mmm—peaches with real whipped cream, ice cream with real whipped cream, strawberry shortcake smothered in real whipped cream... okay, I'll stop tempting you! From now on it'll be easy for you to have real whipped cream whenever you want it. And it'll be as close as your own freezer door! How? My tip is to **make a batch of fresh whipped cream** (I've got the recipe for you on the next page) and **freeze it in dollops about a teaspoon each, on cookie sheets**, until solid. Put the frozen dollops in airtight plastic bags and keep them sealed in the freezer. Then, anytime you want a dollop of real whipped cream, simply take out a piece and put it on your treat. It'll thaw in just a few minutes, and your family and guests will be left wondering where you ever got the time to whip it up and make them feel special. It's really easy! Just make it once, and have it on hand for weeks for topping lots of goodies.

Real Whipped Cream Dollops

about 24 dollops

Fresh whipped cream anytime you want it—with so little work! WOW! A tip like this is gonna get you at least a thousand cries of "More! More! **OOH it's so GOOD!!**™"

½ pint (8 ounces) heavy cream   2 teaspoons confectioners' sugar

In a medium-sized bowl, whip the cream and the sugar with an electric beater on high speed for 3 to 5 minutes or until the cream forms soft peaks (and holds together like real whipped cream is supposed to!). Spoon heaping teaspoon-sized dollops of the whipped cream onto a cookie sheet lined with waxed paper. Freeze for about 1½ hours, or until solid. Transfer the dollops to a plastic bag, close tightly, and keep in the freezer until ready to use. Just before serving, remove one dollop per treat and allow to thaw before eating.

NOTE: These will last in the freezer for up to 1 month.

Steaming Mocha Cocoa

8 servings

This is the perfect crowd-pleasing drink to guarantee smiles on the faces of your friends and family.

6 cups water
1½ cups instant hot chocolate mix
3 tablespoons instant coffee
2 cups half-and-half
8 dollops real whipped cream

In a large saucepan, bring the water to a boil; remove from heat. Gradually stir in the hot chocolate mix and the instant coffee until both are completely dissolved. Slowly add the half-and-half and stir until evenly mixed. Ladle into mugs and top with the whipped cream dollops.

NOTE: If you want a richer drink, go ahead and substitute 2 cups heavy cream for the half-and-half.

I've shared my favorite kitchen tips and shortcuts with you, but I'm sure you've got more of your own favorites, too. Here's the perfect place to write them down so that you can keep the best kitchen helpers together on your way to becoming a kitchen hero!

There's still room for more . . .

Index

air freshener, clove and cinnamon, 85
all-in-one breakfast, 151
almonds, in nutty green beans, 188
aluminum foil, 67–68
apples:
 in lower-fat cooking, 37
 seasoning combination for, 59
asparagus, in open-faced chicken Oscar, 122
awesome munchies, 193

baked goods, purchase of, 46
baking mixes, variations for, 135–136
baking powder biscuits, Mom's, 12
baking soda, baking powder, freshness of, 11
banana(s):
 bread, 149
 Foster, 7
 overripe, 147
 seasoning combination for, 59
barbecued potatoes, 150
batters, light, 15
bean(s):
 canned vs. dried, 101
 double delicious chili, 92
 green, seasoning combination for, 59
 nutty green, 188
 soup, quick black, 102
beef:
 canned, 120
 cola roast, 116
 double delicious chili, 92
 meat cuts, 114–115
 seasoning combinations for, 58
 stew, tenderizing tip for, 115
 tomorrow's shepherd's pie, 112–113

beer batter, for pancakes, 136
bell peppers:
 all-in-one breakfast, 151
 as garnishing, 177
biscuit(s):
 bake, Mexican, 106
 mixes, variations for, 136
 Mom's baking powder, 12
black bean soup, quick, 102
black pepper, 60n
blender tomato sauce, 98
boning and cutting, of chicken, 74, 75–76
brand-name foods, 44
bread:
 banana, 149
 cheese on, 162
 crispy croutons, 153
 garlic, 152
 Mexican biscuit bake, 106
 Mom's baking powder biscuits, 12
 stale, 152
bread crumbs:
 alternative ingredients for, 93–94
 Friday night fried fish, 22
 homemade, 154
bread dough:
 refrigerated and frozen, 103–104
 state fair fried, 105
breading, sticky fingers from, 21
broccoli, seasoning combination for, 59
brownies, lower-fat brown sugar, 39
brown sugar, 195
 softening of, 6
buttermilk biscuit bake, Mexican, 106
butterscotch tea, zesty, 196

Index

cabbage, seasoning combination for, 59
cake:
  mix, variations for, 135–136
  pineapple upside-down, 137
  stale, 168
candy, as hot drink flavoring, 195
carrots, seasoning combination for, 59
cauliflower, pickled, 167
cereal:
  awesome munchies, 193
  as bread crumb substitute, 93, 94
  hodgepodge snack, 192
cheese:
  all-in-one breakfast, 151
  and ham quiche, 163
  and ham salad, spicy, 146
  leftover, 161–162
  and macaroni pie, 110
  open-faced chicken Oscar, 122
cherries, in orange blossom surprises, 179
cherry tomatoes, as garnishing, 177
chicken:
  boning and cutting of, 74, 75–76
  canned, 120
  crispy, 95
  fruity marinated, breasts, 165
  Oscar, open-faced, 122
  rolling pins in preparation of, 81
  Russian, 77
  seasoning combinations for, 58
  soup, as cold medicine, 29–30
  soup, Mom's, 31
  strips, Oriental, 16
  tomato soup, quick, 10
chili, double delicious, 92
chocolate:
  frozen rocky road sandwiches, 190
  in hot drinks, 195
  mint sipper, 196
  steaming mocha cocoa, 199
  sundae sauce, 182
cleaning shortcuts, 83–85
clove and cinnamon air freshener, 85
cocoa, steaming mocha, 199
coffee:
  gelatin, 171
  Irish, 196
  leftover, 170
  liqueur, 194–195
  steaming mocha cocoa, 199
coffeemakers, cleaning of, 84–85
cola roast, 116
color and creativity, 175–178
convenience foods, 117–118
cookie(s):
  crumbs, 140
  cups, 82
  pie crust, 141
  sugar, 71
  zucchini, 28
cookie cutters, homemade, 70
cooking sprays, xiii
corn, seasoning combination for, 59
Cornish hens, wrapped-up, 69
coupon clipping, 44
cracker(s):
  awesome munchies, 193
  crumbs, as bread crumb substitute, 93–94
  graham, in frozen rocky road sandwiches, 190
cranberries, seasoning combination for, 60
crispy chicken, 95
croutons, crispy, 153
crust, cookie pie, 141
cucumbers, pickled, 166, 167
cutting and boning, of chicken, 74, 75–76

deep fryers, 17
defrosting, refrigerator, 54
deglazing, 138
desserts:
  brownies, lower-fat brown sugar, 39
  cookie cups, 82
  fruit trifle, 169
  ice cream sundae bars, 180–181
  lower-fat ingredients in, 37–38
  peanut butter cup surprises, 108
  pineapple upside-down cake, 137
  sugar cookies, 71
  trifles, 168
  zucchini cookies, 28

Index

dessert toppings, 180–181
   chocolate sundae sauce, 182
deviled eggs, perfect, 33
dishwashers, 84
double-batch cooking, 90–91
double delicious chili, 92
dough, bread:
   refrigerated and frozen, 103–104
   state fair fried, 105
drinks:
   banana milkshake, 147
   flavored milk, 189
   hot, 194–195, 196

egg(s):
   all-in-one breakfast, 151
   hard-boiled, 4
   in lower-fat cooking, 38
   perfect deviled, 33
   raw vs. hard-boiled, 32
   salad, perfect, 5
   storage of, 53
equipment, efficient use of, 80–81
extracts, 194

fast French onion soup, 14
fat, *see* lower-fat
fire extinguishers, 18–19, 49
fish:
   canned, 120, 121
   Friday night fried, 22
   seasoning combinations for, 58
flavor-packed fruit punch, 185
French glaze(d), 138
   chicken, 139
French onion soup, fast, 14
Friday night fried fish, 22
fried foods, 17–19
fried rice, vegetable, 119
frozen foods:
   bananas, 147–148
   bread doughs, 103
   shopping for, 45
   storage of, 61, 62, 63
   temperature for, 61
   tomato paste, 8–9
   TV dinners, 155–156, 157
frozen rocky road sandwiches, 190

fruit:
   canned, juice from, 164
   and cheese, 162
   as garnishing, 178
   punch, flavor-packed, 185
   seasoning combinations for, 59–60
   trifle, 169
   see also specific fruits
fruity marinated chicken breasts, 165

garlic:
   bread, 152
   mincing of, 99
   pizza, Italian, 100
gelatin, coffee, 171
glaze:
   chicken, 139
   French, 138
graham crackers, in frozen rocky
   road sandwiches, 190
greens, as garnishing, 177
grocery shopping, 43–46

ham and cheese:
   quiche, 163
   salad, spicy, 146
hard-boiled eggs, 4
   spin test for raw vs., 32
health, and food storage, 61
hens, wrapped-up Cornish, 69
herbs and spices, 55–56
   food and herb complements, 56–57
   organization of, 47–48
   seasoning combinations, 58–60
hodgepodge snack, 192
homemade bread crumbs, 154
honey, as hot drink flavoring, 195
hot peppers:
   fresh chunky Tex-Mex salsa, 36
   handling of, 34–35

ice cream sundae bars, 180–181
ice cubes and molds, 183–184
Irish coffee, 196
Italian garlic pizza, 100

juice:
   from canned fruit, 164
   lemon, getting the most from, 23

Index

kitchen:
    fires in, 18–19
    organization of, 47–49
knives:
    organization and storage of, 47
    purchase and care of, 50–52

leftovers, 145
    bananas, 147
    bread, 152
    cake, 168
    cheese, 161–162
    coffee, 170
    pasta, 158–159
    pickle juice, 166
    potatoes, 150
    refrigeration of, 53
    storage of, 78–79
lemons, 23–24
    flavor-packed fruit punch, 185
lemony tartar sauce, 25
linguine salad, Oriental, 160
liqueur, coffee, 194–195
lower-fat:
    brown sugar brownies, 39
    ingredients, 37–38

macaroni and cheese pie, 110
maple syrup, as hot drink flavoring, 195
marshmallows, in frozen rocky road sandwiches, 190
measurement equivalents, 65–66
measuring cups, sticky waste in, 107
meat:
    canned, 120–121
    loaves, muffin tin, 125
    with pasta, 159
    tenderizing of, 81, 114–115
meat cuts, choice and preparation of, 114–115
Mexican biscuit bake, 106
microwaving, of potatoes, 150
milk:
    flavored, 189
    shakes, 147, 189
mint chocolate sipper, 196
mocha cocoa, steaming, 199
moist heat, 114

Mom's baking powder biscuits, 12
Mom's chicken soup, 31
moo juicers, 189
muffin tin meat loaves, 125

nuts:
    fried, 187
    toasted, 186
    see also peanuts
nutty green beans, 188

odors, kitchen, 85
oil:
    frying with, 17–19
    in handling of hot peppers, 34–35
one-dish meals, 111
    tomorrow's shepherd's pie, 112–113
onions:
    all-in-one breakfast, 151
    green, as garnishing, 177
    peeling with fewer tears, 13
    pickled, 167
    soup, fast French, 14
    storage of, 72
    strings, 73
open-faced chicken Oscar, 122
orange(s):
    blossom surprises, 179
    flavor-packed fruit punch, 185
    seasoning combination for, 59
organization, of kitchen, 47–49
Oriental chicken strips, 16
Oriental pasta salad, 160

packaged foods, xiv
    creative baking with, 135–136
    storage of, 48
pancakes, from biscuit mix, 136
parsley, as garnishing, 177
pasta:
    leftover, 158–159
    macaroni and cheese pie, 110
    quick preparation of, 109
    salad, Oriental, 160
    seasoning combinations for, 59
peach(es):
    seasoning combination for, 59
    trifle, 169

Index

peanut butter cup surprises, 108
peanuts:
  awesome munchies, 193
  frozen rocky road sandwiches, 190
  hodgepodge snack, 192
pears, seasoning combination for, 60
peas, seasoning combination for, 59
pepper, black, 60n
peppers, bell:
  all-in-one breakfast, 151
  as garnishing, 177
peppers, hot:
  fresh chunky Tex-Mex salsa, 36
  handling of, 34–35
perfect deviled eggs, 33
perfect egg salad, 5
pickle juice, leftover, 166
"pickle me silly" tips, 167
pie:
  crust, cookie, 141
  macaroni and cheese, 110
  tomorrow's shepherd's, 112–113
pineapple:
  flavor-packed fruit punch, 185
  fruity marinated chicken breasts, 165
  trifle, 169
  upside-down cake, 137
pizza, 129–130
  Italian garlic, 100
  quick and easy, 131
popsicle sticks, banana, 147
pork, seasoning combinations for, 58
portions, xiii
potato(es):
  all-in-one breakfast, 151
  leftover, 150
  seasoning combinations for, 59
  tomorrow's shepherd's pie, 112–113
potato chips, as bread crumb substitute, 93, 94
pots and pans:
  double uses for, 80
  organization of, 47
poultry, seasoning combinations for, 58
pretzels, in awesome munchies, 193
prune purée, in lower-fat cooking, 37–38

pudding, in frozen rocky road sandwiches, 190
punch, flavor-packed fruit, 185

quiche, ham and cheese, 163

raisins, in hodgepodge snack, 192
refrigerators:
  care of, 53–54
  leftovers stored in, 78, 79
  temperature in, 61
rice:
  seasoning combinations for, 59
  vegetable fried, 119
Russian chicken, 77

salad:
  Oriental pasta, 160
  pasta, 158
  perfect egg, 5
  spicy ham and cheese, 146
salsa, fresh chunky Tex-Mex, 36
sandwiches, frozen rocky road, 190
sauce:
  blender tomato, 98
  cheese in, 161
  chocolate sundae, 182
  fresh chunky Tex-Mex salsa, 36
  lemony tartar, 25
scallions, as garnishing, 177
seasoning combinations, 58–60
  see also herbs and spices
seeds:
  fried, 187
  toasted, 186
serving sizes, xiii
shellfish, seasoning combinations for, 58
shepherd's pie, tomorrow's, 112–113
shopping lists, 43, 44
snack mixes, 191
  awesome munchies, 193
  hodgepodge, 192
soup, 126–127
  black bean, quick, 102
  cheese in, 161
  chicken, as cold medicine, 29–30
  chicken tomato, quick, 10

Index

soup (*continued*)
  fast French onion, 14
  Mom's chicken, 31
  pasta in, 159
  vegetable, quick, 128
spaghetti salad, Oriental, 160
spicy ham and cheese salad, 146
spinach, seasoning combination for, 59
spoilage, 78, 79
squash, seasoning combination for, 59
state fair fried dough, 105
steaming mocha cocoa, 199
storage, 61–64
  of herbs and spices, 55, 60*n*
  of leftovers, 78–79
  of onions, 72
  refrigerator for, 53–54
strawberry(ies), 132–133
  sauce, summer, 134
  seasoning combination for, 60
sugar, brown:
  cookies, 71
  softening of, 6
  varieties of, 195
summer squash, seasoning combination for, 59
summer strawberry sauce, 134

tartar sauce, lemony, 25
tea, zesty butterscotch, 196
temperatures:
  for cheese dishes, 161–162
  for deep frying, 17
  food spoilage and, 78, 79
  for refrigerated and frozen foods, 61
time-saving tips, 109, 123–124, 126–127
toast, 152
tomatoes, 96–97
  cherry, as garnishing, 177
  chicken soup, quick, 10
  double delicious chili, 92
  sauce, blender, 98
  seasoning combination for, 59
tomato paste cubes, 8–9
tomorrow's shepherd's pie, 112–113
toppings:
  cheese, 162
  dessert, 180–181
trifle(s), 168
  fruit, 169
TV dinners, 155–156, 157

upside-down cake, pineapple, 137
utensils, organization of, 47

vegetable(s):
  disguising of, 26–27
  fried rice, 119
  seasoning combination for, 59
  soup, quick, 128
  see also specific vegetables

whipped cream, 197
  dollops, real, 198
  frozen rocky road sandwiches, 190
  in hot drinks, 195
wrapped-up Cornish hens, 69

zesty butterscotch tea, 196
zucchini cookies, 28

Mr. Food®

Can Help You Be A Kitchen Hero!

Let **Mr. Food®** make your life easier with
Quick, No-Fuss Recipes and Helpful Kitchen Tips for

*Family Dinners   Soups and Salads   Pot Luck Dishes
Barbecues   Special Brunches   Unbelievable Desserts
...and that's just the beginning!*

There are easy, updated versions of Mama's specialties in **Mr. Food®** *Cooks Like Mama*, new twists on American classics in **Mr. Food®** *Cooks Real American*, and scrumptious treats in **Mr. Food®** *Makes Dessert* and **Mr. Food®** *'s Favorite Cookies*. And now, with the incredibly simple **Mr. Food®** *'s Quick and Easy Side Dishes*, the barbecuing bonanza in **Mr. Food®** *Grills It All in a Snap*, and the gold mine of helpful hints in **Mr. Food®** *'s Fun Kitchen Tips and Shortcuts (and Recipes, Too!)*, **it's all here!** All of **Mr. Food®**'s recipes use readily-available ingredients, and can be made in no time! So, don't miss out! Join in on the fun!

It's so simple to share in all the
OOH IT'S SO GOOD!!™

✂--

TITLE	PRICE	QUANTITY		
A. **Mr. Food®** Cooks Like Mama	@ $12.95 ea.	x _____	=	$_____
B. The **Mr. Food®** Cookbook, *OOH IT'S SO GOOD!!*™	@ $12.95 ea.	x _____	=	$_____
C. **Mr. Food®** Cooks Chicken	@ $ 9.95 ea.	x _____	=	$_____
D. **Mr. Food®** Cooks Pasta	@ $ 9.95 ea.	x _____	=	$_____
E. **Mr. Food®** Makes Dessert	@ $ 9.95 ea.	x _____	=	$_____
F. **Mr. Food®** Cooks Real American	@ $14.95 ea.	x _____	=	$_____
G. **Mr. Food®**'s Favorite Cookies	@ $11.95 ea.	x _____	=	$_____
H. **Mr. Food®**'s Quick and Easy Side Dishes	@ $11.95 ea.	x _____	=	$_____
I. **Mr. Food®** Grills It All in a Snap	@ $11.95 ea.	x _____	=	$_____
J. **Mr. Food®**'s Fun Kitchen Tips and Shortcuts (and Recipes, Too!)	@ $11.95 ea.	x _____	=	$_____

Send payment to: **Mr. Food®**
P.O. Box 696
Holmes, PA 19043

Book Total $_____

+$2.95 Postage & Handling *First Copy*
AND
$1 Ea. Add'l. Copy
(Canadian Orders Add Add'l. $2.00 *Per Copy*) $_____

Name_____

Street_____

Subtotal $_____

City_____ State_____ Zip_____

Method of Payment: ☐ Check or Money Order Enclosed
☐ Credit Card: ☐ Visa ☐ MasterCard: Expiration Date _____
Signature_____

Less $1.00 per book if ordering 3 or more books with this order $-_____

Add Applicable Sales Tax (FL Residents Only) $_____

Total in U.S. Funds $_____

Account #:
☐☐☐☐☐☐☐☐☐☐☐☐

Please allow 4 to 6 weeks for delivery.   BKI1

Make Your Kitchen a Pizzeria

Problem: It's late at night and you've got a craving for pizza. "No problem!" you think—till you find out that the local pizzeria is closed and you're out of frozen pizza. **You've got the pizza "munchies" and you don't really want to go to bed without that pizza!** No problem!

No More Pizza "Munchies"!

If a "traditional" pizza just can't be had, then make your own. It's quick and easy. And you can be adventurous! Here are the basics:

- Start with a bread base. Use anything from Italian bread to English muffins, bagels, or even pita bread.
- Next come the sauce and toppings. Traditional pizza has a rich red sauce, but you can really get daring and make it unique. Toppings could be anything from cooked meats to different kinds of cheese and veggies. But why not try these:
- Make a "pizza" of ham and Swiss cheese slices, and mustard on an English muffin.
- Scrambled eggs on a buttered bagel, topped with American cheese and dill. It's a breakfast pizza!
- Spread some bottled pesto sauce on Italian bread and top with sliced black olives and Muenster cheese.
- Try some chunks of tuna fish and tomatoes topped with Havarti cheese on pita bread for a gourmet-type pizza.

continued

Time and Money Savers

- What about leftover spaghetti and sauce on an English muffin, topped with pepperoni and mozzarella cheese?
- Go exotic and make a Greek pizza: Put some thinly sliced cooked lamb on a pita bread and top with herb cheese.

After you assemble your creation, follow the cooking instructions in the following recipe.